The Dynamics of

Preaching

Other books in the
Ministry Dynamics for a New Century series
WARREN W. WIERSBE, series editor

Other books by Warren Wiersbe

The Dynamics of
Preaching

WARREN W. WIERSBE

Baker Books

A Division of Baker Book House Co
Grand Rapids, Michigan 49516

Published by Baker Books
a division of Baker Book House Company
P.O. Box 6287, Grand Rapids, MI 49516-6287

Second printing, March 2000

Printed in the United States of America

Library of Congress Cataloging-in-Publication Data

Wiersbe, Warren W.
  The dynamics of preaching / Warren W. Wiersbe.
      p.   cm. — (Ministry dynamics for a new century)
  Includes bibliographical references and index.
  ISBN 0-8010-9089-X
  1. Preaching. I. Title II. Series.
BV4211.2.W46 1999
251—dc21   99–16361

For current information about all releases from Baker Book House, visit our web site:
                     http://www.bakerbooks.com

Contents

Series Preface

The purpose of the Ministry Dynamics series is to provide both experienced and beginning pastors with concise information that will help them do the task of ministry with efficiency, fruitfulness, and joy.

The word *ministry* means "service," something that Jesus exemplified in his own life and that he expects us to practice in our lives. No matter what our title or position, we are in the church to serve God's people. The word *dynamics* is not used as an equivalent of "power" but as a reminder that nothing stands still in Christian ministry. If it does, it dies. True biblical ministry involves constant challenge and change, learning and growth, and how we handle these various elements determines the strength and success of the work that we do.

The emphasis in this series is on practical service founded on basic principles and not on passing fads. Some older ministers need to catch up with the present while newer ministers need to catch up on the past. We all can learn much from each other if only we're honest enough to admit it and humble enough to accept each other's counsel.

I began pastoring in 1950 and over the years have seen many changes take place in local church ministry, from bus ministries and house churches to growth groups and megachurches. Some of the changes have been good and are now integrated into God's work in many churches. But some ideas that attracted national attention decades ago now exist only on the pages of forgotten books in used-book stores. How quickly today's exciting headlines become tomorrow's footnotes! "Test everything. Hold on to the good" (1 Thess. 5:21).

An ancient anonymous prayer comes to mind:

> From the cowardice that shrinks from new truth,
> From the laziness that is content with half-
>   truths,
> From the arrogance that thinks it knows all
>   truth,
>   O God of truth, deliver us!

Our desire is that both the seasoned servant and the new seminary graduate will find encouragement and enlightenment from the Ministry Dynamics series.

Warren W. Wiersbe

Introduction

Just about everything useful ever written about preaching has attempted to answer two questions: What good is preaching? and What is *good* preaching? This book is no exception.

More than one preacher has asked himself (or the Lord), *What good is preaching?* Preaching worked for the apostles in the first century and for a few "great preachers" in succeeding centuries, but does it still work today? Do I have the right to expect people to listen to the sermons I preach? If God promises to bless the preaching of his Word, why don't we see more changed lives and dynamic fellowship in our churches?

What is *good* preaching? is the question that gnaws away at the heart of the devoted preacher who wants to give God the very best. Is preaching good because it produces visible results or because parishoners compliment us or because church attendance increases? Was a sermon good because some people got angry and left the church? It's not easy to measure ministry, especially the ministry of speaking sounds into air, invisible words that only God can propel effectively into needy hearts.

In the spirit of the apostle Paul, expressed in Philippians 3:12, I want to review the basic principles of homiletics and help both beginning preachers and veteran ministers apply them to their own preaching situations today. During nearly half a century of preaching, teaching, and writing, I've followed the counsel of a bit of doggerel that a seminary professor dropped into a dull lecture one morning and thereby rescued what might have become a totally wasted hour:

> Methods are many, principles are few;
> Methods always change, principles never do.

The emphasis in this book will be on unchanging principles and not on passing fads.

Henry Thoreau wrote on the first page of *Walden:* "In most books, the *I*, or first person, is omitted; in this it will be retained. . . ." Students in the classroom and pastors in seminars have often asked about my personal approach to preaching, not because my way is the only way or even the best way, but because they were interested in knowing what has worked for me. You must find the approach that best works for you. But I hope you will find in these pages a hint or two that will help make your preaching more enjoyable and effective.

We Preach

Woe to me if I do not preach the gospel!

1 Corinthians 9:16

At some point in your ministry, you may have asked yourself the same questions many of us have asked ourselves: *Why all this emphasis on* preaching? *What is there about preaching that makes it so important to the ministry of the church?*

We really need to answer those questions, because if we don't sincerely believe in the importance of preaching, we won't be able to do our best and will be functioning in a religious masquerade. If there's one thing preaching demands it's authenticity.

The Experts Speak

Let's begin with some of the respected homileticians. John A. Broadus ranks at the top. His *Preparation and*

Delivery of Sermons, first published in 1870, is a classic text in the field. The book opens with this declaration: "The great appointed means of spreading the good tidings of salvation through Christ is preaching words—spoken, whether to the individual, or to the assembly."[1] In short, preaching is important.

Seven years later, Phillips Brooks gave his famous *Lectures on Preaching* at Yale Divinity School. He wasn't five minutes into his first lecture when he said:

> I cannot begin, then, to speak to you who are preparing for the work of preaching, without congratulating you most earnestly upon the prospect that lies before you. . . . Let us rejoice with one another that in a world where there are a great many good and happy things for men to do, God has given us the best and happiest, and made us preachers of His Truth.[2]

John Watson (whose pen name was Ian Maclaren) gave the Yale Lectures in 1896. He opened his first lecture by reminding his hearers that "the most critical and influential event in the religious week is the sermon."[3] Preaching is not only important; it's *critically* important.

But perhaps these ancient texts are prejudiced. Back in those days people didn't have television sets and computers and weren't plugged into the Internet; so let's turn to some recent books on preaching such as *Preaching and Preachers* by Dr. D. Martyn Lloyd-Jones. The Doctor immediately nails his colors to the mast by calling chapter one "The Primacy of Preaching." In the very first paragraph he says that "the work of preaching is the highest and the greatest and the most glorious calling to which anyone can ever be called."[4]

That's quite a claim for a vocation that television comics parody and the general public ignores. Let's confess that not every preacher feels "high and great and glorious" after preaching on Sunday. More than once we've gone home wondering if we should spend less time preparing sermons and more time attending committee meetings or organizing small groups. But Dr. Lloyd-Jones is right: Preaching God's Word is a high and glorious calling.

We turn next to Dr. John R. W. Stott's *Between Two Worlds: The Art of Preaching in the Twentieth Century* and find that the first chapter is entitled "The Glory of Preaching." Dr. Stott writes, "That preaching is central and distinctive to Christianity has been recognized throughout the Church's long and colorful story, even from the beginning."[5] Preaching is critically important and preaching is central. The moderns agree with the ancients!

Finally, Dr. Brian Chapell opens the first chapter of his book *Christ-Centered Preaching* with the caption "The Nobility of Preaching"; and he quotes with emphatic approval Dr. Robert G. Rayburn's statement to seminary students, "Christ is the only King of your studies, but homiletics is the queen."[6] God save the queen!

The Stock Reasons

The people who sit in the pews probably haven't read Lloyd-Jones, Stott, or Chapell. Like too many church members, perhaps they still believe the old deacons' tale that pastors are supposed to wait on tables and not devote themselves continually to prayer and the ministry of the Word (Acts 6:1–4). It may not really matter to them how the pastor preaches on Sunday just as long as the machinery of the church keeps running, the bills are paid, and the people keep attending.

But preaching is important! Whether you read the Bible, the recent books on preaching, or the old homiletical classics, you find this conviction emphasized repeatedly: Preaching God's Word is the most important thing the minister does. Let's review the stock reasons why preaching is important and perhaps question them a bit.

Preaching is important because God has ordained preaching! But why *preaching* and not some other approach to sharing the Word? After all, we're preaching to people who live in a media-mad world, and some of them have the attention span of a nervous two-year-old.

How shall they hear without a preacher? Well, they could eavesdrop on a Christian conversation, which is the way John Bunyan heard the gospel. Or they might watch a Christian video or a drama.

Paul commanded us to preach the Word. So we're back to square one: why *preaching* and not some other method?

Preaching is what builds the church. But as important as preaching is, every minister knows that it takes more than a strong pulpit to build a strong church. Preaching is certainly a key factor, but it isn't the only factor.

The Real Reason

According to the Book of Acts, the first-century church was faithful to share God's message in many different ways. They preached the gospel (5:42; 8:4, 12, 25, 35, 40, and others) and God was faithful to bless his Word. The apostles persuaded people (18:13), taught them (11:26; 15:35), explained and interpreted the Scriptures (15:12; 17:3; 18:26), refuted arguments

(18:28), gave personal witness to Christ (3:15; 5:32), and confounded their adversaries in debates (9:22). And while the apostles and other church leaders were doing these things, the believers were witnessing about Jesus—"gossiping the gospel"—so that day after day God was able to add new believers to the church (4:1, 20, 29, 31; 5:20, 40; 11:19).

All these modes of witnessing have one thing in common: They were done by believing people whose Spirit-filled lives and gracious speech the Spirit used to spread the good news. This, I've concluded, is the crux of the matter and explains why God has ordained the preaching of the Word. *The Word that became flesh when the Son of God came to earth* (John 1:14) *must again and again "become flesh" through his people as they proclaim God's message.* This is especially true for those of us who have been chosen to preach as ministers of the Word.[7]

In short, effective preaching is personal; it's people talking to people about something that is really important to them. Preachers must be more than *heralds* who declare the King's message or *teachers* who explain it. They must also be *witnesses* who boldly testify to what the message means to them personally and loving *shepherds* who skillfully apply God's truth to the lives of the people they serve and know.

If all we want to accomplish in a message is the heralding and explaining of the Word, why not play sermon tapes from gifted preachers and spend our sermon preparation time playing golf? Because God's people need to hear a *personal* witness to the power of God's Word, a witness who helps them apply God's truth to their own lives so they can be better disciples. We need in our pulpits witnesses who have learned and lived the Word and shepherds who know their people and how to help them from the Scriptures.

Yes, preaching must be personal. The Word must be "made flesh." To expand on the well-known definition of preaching from Phillips Brooks: Preaching is the communicating of divine truth through human personality to human personality for the purpose of building up God's people to the glory of God.[8]

What Happens When We Preach?

When you consider some of the images of preaching found in Scripture, you get a better understanding of what God has called preachers to do. "I am watching over My word to perform it," God promised his prophet (Jer. 1:12 NASB), but what is he performing while we're proclaiming?

To begin with, *he's letting in the light.* "The unfolding of your words gives light; it gives understanding to the simple" (Ps. 119:130). God's "Let there be light" was not only the beginning of the old creation (Gen. 1:1–3), but it's also the beginning of a new creation when sinners hear the Word and trust Christ (2 Cor. 4:6). The darkness of sin is dispelled and the face of Jesus Christ is seen radiating the glory of God. What a thrill it is to hear the new believer exclaim, "I was blind but now I see!" (John 9:25).

God is also *planting the seed of his truth.* "The seed is the word of God" and the soil represents the human heart (Luke 8:11–15). When the disciples saw that great crowd on the shore listening to Jesus teaching from the boat (Luke 8:4), they probably concluded that their ministry was a great success; but in his parable, Jesus pointed out that three-fourths of the seed sown would produce no lasting fruit. In spite of that, God is still watching over his Word and accomplishing his purposes, and "at the proper time we will reap a harvest if we do not give up" (Gal. 6:9).

The preaching of the Word means *dispensing God's medicine to the spiritually sick*. "He sent forth his word and healed them" (Ps. 107:20). The preacher always feels gratified and gives praise to God when a worshiper says after a service, "Pastor, I'm scheduled to come in to see you this week, but I don't have to come. The sermon this morning solved my problem and met the need." The Word was sent out and the Lord brought the healing. Apart from the ministry of the Holy Spirit, our work as spiritual physicians would be impossible; for only the Spirit fully knows the need of every heart and how to apply the medicine.

Through faithful preaching, the Lord brings *cleansing to defiled lives*. "You are already clean because of the word I have spoken to you," Jesus assured his disciples (John 15:3). We live in a dirty world, and even the most cautious saints find themselves picking up and harboring thoughts and feelings that are foreign to the Christian life. The experience of worship, which includes hearing the Scriptures read, sung, and preached, is our Lord's way of cleansing his church "by the washing with water through the word" (Eph. 5:26).

There are times when preaching means *wielding the sword against the enemy*. God's Word is the sharp "sword of the Spirit" (Eph. 6:17; Heb. 4:12) that penetrates and wounds to bring healing. Every preacher longs for the experience Peter had on the day of Pentecost when the people were "cut to the heart" and asked, "Brothers, what shall we do?" (Acts 2:37). What David said of Goliath's sword, we can say of the sword of God's Word: "There is none like it" (1 Sam. 21:9).

Perhaps the image of preaching that we think of most frequently is that of *serving spiritual food to God's children,* because God's family lives on God's truth (Matt. 4:4). We prepare a sermon as a cook prepares a meal, and we seek to serve it in such a way that the listeners will enjoy the vegetables as well as the dessert. We want everyone to say with Jeremiah, "When your words came, I ate them; they were my joy and my heart's delight, for I bear your name" (Jer. 15:16). We long for our people to have the ravenous appetite of the newborn baby (1 Peter 2:2), while at the same time growing out of the milk diet and into the menu of solid food (1 Cor. 3:1–4; Heb. 5:9–14).

God's Word is like gold and silver (Ps. 119:14, 72, 127, 162), and when we declare this Word in preaching, we're *investing spiritual wealth in the lives of God's people.* "And the things you have heard me say in the presence of many witnesses entrust to reliable men who will also be qualified to teach others" (2 Tim. 2:2). God had entrusted the truth to Paul (1 Tim. 1:11), who deposited it with Timothy (1 Tim. 6:20). Timothy was obligated to guard the truth and pass it along to others who would in turn teach it to the new generation of believers. We can't reap spiritual dividends if we don't invest the Word in the lives of others.

These are but a selection of the images of preaching found in Scripture, but surely they're sufficient to convince us that it's a good thing to preach and that preaching does good when people hear the Word and put it to work in their lives.

The "Frightful Adventure"

"The witness cannot affirm great truths lightly," wrote the French philosopher Jacques Ellul. "Precisely for this reason preaching is the most frightful adventure. I have no right to make a mistake that makes God a liar."⁹

Preaching the Word is indeed an awesome challenge that ought to frighten both the overconfident and the underprepared. But even when our confidence is in Christ and we've done our best to prepare ourselves and our message, we have to admit that we're unprofitable servants. "And who is equal to such a task?" asked Paul, who then gave the assuring answer: "Not that we are competent in ourselves to claim anything for ourselves, but our competence comes from God. He has made us competent as ministers of a new covenant" (2 Cor. 2:16; 3:5–6). And the apostle might have added, "The one who calls you is faithful and he will do it" (1 Thess. 5:24).

The Conclusion of the Matter

The conclusion is simply this: In a world mesmerized by electronic wonders, everything from television to cyberspace, the preaching of the Word of God is still important and is still being blessed by God. Next to Sunday's sermon, the fascinating world of the Internet may seem like a menacing giant; but with the help of God, the sermon becomes the David that slays the giant.

Paul put it this way in 2 Corinthians 10:3–5:

> For though we live in the world, we do not wage war as the world does. The weapons we fight with are not the weapons of the world. On the contrary, they have divine power to demolish strongholds. We demolish arguments and every pretension that sets itself up against the knowledge of God, and we take captive every thought to make it obedient to Christ.

While on holiday in Switzerland, the eminent Scottish preacher Alexander Whyte received a letter from a minister seeking direction about his future. The man was discouraged and admitted that he scarcely knew "how or what to preach." Whyte replied: "Never think of giving up preaching! The angels around the throne envy you your great work."[10]

Yes, the angels would gladly take our places, but they lack the one ingredient that makes preaching credible and powerful: the personal experience of the grace of God. Angels could be eloquent *heralds* of God's truth, but they could never be experienced *witnesses* of the manifold grace of God.

Who is equal to such a task?

Nobody. "But thanks be to God! He gives us the victory through our Lord Jesus Christ" (1 Cor. 15:57).

We believe in God and we believe in preaching and, therefore, *we preach!*

Two
We Preach the Scriptures

Preach the Word.

2 Timothy 4:2

In that neglected Christian classic *The Pilgrim's Progress,* by John Bunyan, we read of Christian going into the House of the Interpreter where he sees a majestic painting.

> Christian saw the painting of a very grave person . . . and this was the fashion of it. It has eyes lifted up to heaven, the best of books in his hand, the law of truth was written upon his lips, the world was behind his back. It stood as if it pleaded with men, and a crown of gold did hang over his head.

In this picture, Bunyan described the ideal minister of the gospel, borrowing most of the imagery from Malachi 2:1–9. *Grave* doesn't mean "solemn" or "somber," the kind of people you see in some of the old Dutch paintings, but rather *serious about his calling and the preaching of the Word of God.* Contrary to the popular caricature of the Puritans, they were a happy people, but they took life seriously. The minister looked up to heaven because that's where he got the insight to understand the Word and the power to preach it effectively, and more than anything else, he wanted to please his Lord in heaven. The world had nothing to offer him, but he had something wonderful to offer to the world; so he stood pleading with lost sinners to be reconciled with God. The crown reminds us of God's promise to faithful ministers: "And when the Chief Shepherd appears, you will receive the crown of glory that will never fade away" (1 Peter 5:4).

The statement that arrests my attention is "the best of books in his hand," referring, of course, to the Bible. The truth in the book in his hand made its way through the faithful pastor's heart to his mouth, for "the law of truth was written upon his lips." He was obeying Paul's familiar injunction, "Preach the Word." And Bunyan may have had Isaiah 8:20 in mind, "To the law and to the testimony! If they do not speak according to this word, they have no light of dawn."

Is That What Preachers Are?

In the previous chapter we considered what God does when we faithfully preach the Word, but we only touched the surface, because there are numerous images of the preacher and preaching in Scripture. Among other things, preachers are:

- *Fishermen*—"Come, follow me . . . and I will make you fishers of men" (Mark 1:17).
- *Ambassadors*—"We are therefore Christ's ambassadors, as though God were making his appeal through us" (2 Cor. 5:20).

- *Witnesses*—"For we cannot help speaking about what we have seen and heard" (Acts 4:20).
- *Sowers and harvesters*—"The harvest is plentiful but the workers are few" (Matt. 9:37; and see John 4:35–38; 1 Cor. 3:5–9).
- *Shepherds*—"Feed my lambs. . . . Take care of my sheep" (John 21:15–16; and see John 10:1–18; Luke 15:3–7).
- *Rescuers*—"snatch others from the fire and save them" (Jude 23; and see Zech. 3:1–4; Prov. 24:11–12).
- *Spiritual parents*—"for in Christ Jesus I became your father through the gospel" (1 Cor. 4:15; and see 1 Thess. 2:7, 11).
- *Priests of God*—"to be a minister of Christ Jesus . . . with the priestly duty of proclaiming the gospel of God" (Rom. 15:16; and see 1 Peter 2:5, 9).
- *Soldiers*—"The weapons we fight with are not the weapons of the world. On the contrary, they have divine power to demolish strongholds" (2 Cor. 10:4; and see 2 Tim. 2:3–4).
- *Heralds of the King*—"Preach [herald] the Word" (2 Tim. 4:2; and see Rom. 10:8; Col. 1:23).
- *Stewards*—"we speak as men approved by God to be entrusted with the gospel" (1 Thess. 2:4; and see 1 Cor. 4:1–7).

The Old Testament has its share of images of ministry, especially in the Book of Jeremiah. Like Ezekiel and John the Baptist, Jeremiah was called from being a priest to being a prophet, and at first he debated the matter with the Lord. After all, it was much easier to serve as a priest: Your needs were met by the gifts of the people, your work was explained in the Law, and your service was pretty much routine. A prophet's work was difficult and dangerous, and you were never sure from one day to another what the Lord would call you to do.

But God assured Jeremiah that he would make him as steady and strong as a pillar and a wall (Jer. 1:18–19), even though his work wouldn't be easy. Jeremiah would have to tear down and root out before he could build up and plant (1:10). By his preaching, he would "turn on the heat" and test the people the way assayers test metal (6:27–30). He would also minister as a physician to people whose religious leaders were giving them false diagnoses and useless remedies (6:14; 8:11, 21–22). Jeremiah was a shepherd to lost sheep (13:17) and a runner against difficult odds (12:5), but he felt like a lamb being led to the slaughter (11:19). Some of us can identify with these images.

These biblical images of ministry—and there are many more—remind us that there are many facets to our work, that all of them are difficult, and none of them are monotonous. Ministry is chock-full of surprising opportunities and challenges that ought to encourage us to grow; but whether we're shepherding the sheep, feeding the family, or pulling brands out of the fire, one thing is sure: *We can't do the job apart from the Word of God.*

The Preacher and the Word

"The Bible is God preaching," says James I. Packer.[1] If we're adequately prepared and the Spirit is at work, we don't preach the Bible so much as allow the Bible to preach through us. Not that we're passive channels, for the personality of the preacher is an important part of the message; but the preacher is a "distributor" rather than a "manufacturer." For this reason, we must be devoted to the Word of God, meditating on it daily, studying it systematically, reading it continually, and always feeding our own souls and preparing to feed our people. "Set your heart upon God's Word!" Charles Spurgeon told his London congregation. "It is the only way to know it thoroughly; let your whole nature be plunged into it as cloth into a dye."[2]

Authority

The authority of the message comes from the Word and not from the approval of people. "Look, as one man the other prophets are predicting success for the king," the guard told the faithful prophet Micaiah. "Let your word agree with theirs, and speak favorably." But the servant of God wasn't interested in winning a popularity contest. "As surely as the LORD lives," he replied, "I can tell him only what my God says" (2 Chron. 18:12–13). Four hundred prophets disagreed with him, but Micaiah's message proved to be accurate. When we're no longer controlled by "Thus saith the Lord!" we start preaching opinions instead of convictions and seek to please ourselves and our listeners instead of pleasing the Lord. "We are not trying to please men," wrote Paul, "but God, who tests our hearts" (1 Thess. 2:4). Without God's truth, what we say to the congregation is only straw, and straw doesn't nourish hungry hearts. "Let the one who has my word speak it faithfully. For what has straw to do with grain?" (Jer. 23:28).

Power

The Word of God not only gives the message authority, but it also gives it power. The Lord went on to say to Jeremiah, "Is not my word like fire . . . and like a hammer that breaks a rock in pieces?" (Jer. 23:29). The same living, powerful Word that brought creation into being also works in the new creation, bringing light into darkness and order out of chaos (2 Cor. 4:3–6). "Our gospel came to you not simply with words, but also with power, with the Holy Spirit and with deep conviction" (1 Thess. 1:5). Speaking words isn't the same as preaching *the* Word, any more than reciting a recipe is the same as serving a meal.

Humility

When we preach the Word faithfully, we're delivered from the kind of homiletical calisthenics that turns preaching into performing and magnifies the minister more than the message. Paul was not only a servant of Christ and the church, but he was also a servant of the gospel (Col. 1:25). When you're mastered by the message, you're not interested in clever outlines and amusing anecdotes. Your only concern is, "Hear the Word of the Lord!"

Integrity

Preaching the Word of God encourages us to live the Word of God so that our message is an honest witness of our own experience of God's truth. "Therefore every scribe who has become a disciple of the kingdom of heaven is like a head of a household, who brings forth out of his treasure things new and old" (Matt. 13:52 NASB). The sequence is logical: We are scribes learning the Word who become disciples obeying the Word and then householders sharing the Word with others. On more than one occasion I've had to interrupt my sermon preparation because the text had convicted me and I had to spend time with the Lord getting my heart right. I could have outlined the passage and preached a sermon, but in God's sight it would have been a mockery and not a message. Scribes who are not disciples become hypocrites.

Confidence

"Faith comes from hearing the message, and the message is heard through the word of Christ" (Rom. 10:17). Unless the Word that we study and prepare works in our own lives and generates faith, the messages we deliver aren't likely to accomplish very much. The LORD says that just as the rain and the snow cause the seeds in the earth to produce life, yielding "seed for the sower and bread for the eater, so is my word that goes out from my mouth: It will not return to me empty, but will accomplish what I desire and achieve the purpose for which I sent it" (Isa. 55:10–11). It's necessary for ministers to be faithful to the Word but we must also have faith in the Word.

"I used to think I should close my Bible and pray for faith," said evangelist Dwight L. Moody, "but I came to see that it was in studying the Word that I was to get faith."[3] If our study of the Bible doesn't increase our own faith, then our preaching of the Bible isn't likely to generate faith in anybody else. Not only must we believe in preaching, but we must also believe in what we preach. "Have faith in God" (Mark 11:22).

Our People and the Word

Only a miracle book like the Bible could meet the varied needs of the people who make up the average congregation, and God help the church whose shepherd feeds the sheep on substitutes. It's doubtful that the most brilliant academic lecturer or the most famous politician or business leader could gather a crowd week by week such as assembles in thousands of sanctuaries to hear the Bible preached. What are people looking for when they come to hear the Word of God expounded?

We live in a deceptive world and people need to hear *"the word of truth"* (Ps. 119:43; Eph. 1:13–14; 2 Tim. 2:15; James 1:18). They need to get their minds cleared of lies and their eyes focused on the real world, which is the "world" described in Scripture. Mark Twain said that a lie runs around the world while truth is putting on her shoes, and that was before the development of television and satellites. The average American watches thirty hours of television a week and thinks he's seeing the real world but he isn't. Television is an entertainment medium that manufactures its own world, invents its own rules, and defends its own values.

Our people live in a difficult and demanding world and need to hear *"the word of his grace"* (Acts 20:32). Unless we are bivocational pastors, we probably spend more time in the stands than on the field, but our people confront the brutal realities of life day after day. The old adage is still true: Be kind, for everyone you meet is fighting a battle. It isn't enough just to be saved by God's grace; we also need to live by God's grace, like Paul who confessed, "But by the grace of God I am what I am" (1 Cor. 15:10). He depended on God's grace for everything from his serving (1 Cor. 15:10) and suffering (2 Cor. 12:9) to his singing and speaking (Col. 3:16; 4:6). As we preach, we must remind our hurting people that the God they worship is "the God of all grace" (1 Peter 5:10) and that "from the fullness of his grace we have all received one blessing after another" (John 1:16).

The world we live in is a defiled world and God's people are finding it more and more difficult to stay clean. For that reason we all need *"the word of righteousness"*

(Heb. 5:13 NASB), which not only reveals God's righteousness to us but enables us to experience "training in righteousness" (2 Tim. 3:16) that makes us more like Jesus (Rom. 8:29). Like a mirror, the Word shows us where we're dirty (James 1:22–25); and like water, the Word cleanses us in the inner person (Eph. 5:25–27), and we are sanctified by God's truth (John 17:17).

Finally, the people we serve live in a divisive and competitive world and need to hear *"the word of reconciliation"* (2 Cor. 5:19 NASB). George Bernard Shaw suggested that if the other planets are inhabited, they're using the earth as their insane asylum; and there are times when it seems he was right. At home, on the campus, in the marketplace, and even at church, relationships are strained and often shattered, and the result is pain in the heart that brings even more pressure into the life. Only Jesus can reconcile people to God, to themselves, and to others around them. God's purpose in this world is "to bring all things in heaven and on earth together under one head, even Christ" (Eph. 1:10), and that's why we preach "the word of reconciliation."

The Word of God will do all these things and more if God's people will hear it, believe it, and obey it. God's Word is *"the word of faith"* (Rom. 10:8); it releases its power only when believed and obeyed. "For no word from God shall be void of power" (Luke 1:37 ASV). God's commandments are still God's enablements because his Word is *"the word of His power"* (Heb. 1:3 NASB).

"Always the Word"

A pastor friend of mine chose as the motto for his church, "Always the Word," a ministry statement that is both biblical and doable. Whether the children's choir was singing, a missionary was reporting, or the pastor was preaching, in that congregation it was always the Word.

No one sermon can accomplish everything that needs to be done in a church, and the cumulative result of our preaching week after week can't be measured accurately. Only God sees what's happening in the hearts of the people to whom we preach and for whom we pray, but there's usually sufficient blessing to encourage us to keep on sharing God's truth. But even if there isn't the kind of fruit we long to see, we're confident that the Word will accomplish God's purposes and "at the proper time we will reap a harvest if we do not give up" (Gal. 6:9).

We Preach Christ

> In the New Testament we are confronted with a religious life in which everything is determined by Christ.
>
> James Denney
> *Jesus and the Gospel*

The Scriptures are "the word of Christ" (Col. 3:16), which implies that the faithful preaching of the Scriptures means "preaching Christ." It also means following the example of our Savior as he ministered on the Emmaus road: "And beginning with Moses and all the Prophets, he explained to them what was said in all the Scriptures concerning himself" (Luke 24:27). All Scripture is inspired and all Scripture bears witness to Jesus Christ.

What It Is to Preach Christ

Preaching Christ means much more than merely mentioning his name occasionally in the sermon or quoting something he said. I suggest that preaching Christ means proclaiming the Word of God in such a way that Jesus Christ is clearly presented in all the fullness of his person and the greatness of his work. He is glorified as the eternal Son of God, Creator, Savior of the world, Lord of history, and Head of the church. He is magnified as the heart of every Christian doctrine and the motivation for every Christian duty. When Christ is preached, the Holy Spirit can use the message to enable God's people to respond to Christ with greater love, faith, and obedience and to draw unbelievers to Christ in saving faith.

Obviously we don't include all of this magnificent theology in every sermon or even in any one sermon, because this definition of preaching Christ is not a checklist. It's really more of a compass to keep us from going on detours. No matter what biblical text we expound, our desire to preach Christ will compel us to use that text to direct our listeners' minds and hearts to Jesus Christ and Calvary's cross. "If a man can preach one sermon without mentioning Christ's name in it," warned Charles Spurgeon, "it ought to be his last, and certainly the last that any Christian ought to go to hear him preach."[1]

When we're preaching an Old Testament text that may not have obvious Messianic implications, it's easy to talk about God in general and ignore Jesus Christ. We're especially vulnerable when we preach from Old Testament narrative or from the poetic books. One of my students told me it was "against the rules" to bring New Testament theology into Old Testament passages, and I asked him if Philip the evangelist knew that rule when he witnessed to the Ethiopian treasurer. "Then Philip began with that very passage of Scripture [Isaiah 53] and told him the good news about Jesus" (Acts 8:35). Certainly we want to know what the Old Testament passages meant to the original hearers or readers, but we don't stay there.

Preaching Christ Is
What the Church Needs

"Jesus Christ is the same yesterday and today and forever" (Heb. 13:8). He is the Christ of history (yesterday), because the faith that we profess and preach is founded on fact. But he is also the Christ of experience (today), ministering to his people today. Otherwise, the church is simply a museum where we have embalmed the past and we assemble once a week to admire the corpse. From the throne in heaven, the living Christ ministers to and through his people, accomplishing his purposes on earth (Heb. 13:20–21). Finally, he is the Christ of prophecy (forever) who will fulfill his eternal purposes and answer the prayers of his people, "Thy kingdom come."

Yesterday

We preach the Christ of history. If Jesus Christ is not an authentic historic person, the Son of God who came in sinless humanity, then the message we preach is a meaningless myth. If he did not live on this earth, if he was not "crucified under Pontius Pilate," if he did not rise from the dead and ascend to heaven, then we have no message to preach. The faith of the church is built on the historic witness of the apostles who knew him personally. They heard him speak, saw him perform miracles, touched him, ate with him, saw him die, met him after his resurrection, and watched him return to heaven (John 15:27; 20:30–31; 21:24–25; Acts 1:1–11; 1 Cor. 15:1–8; 2 Peter 1:16–21; 1 John 1:1–4). Jesus

Christ was so much a part of human history that Dr. Luke was able to research the facts and write an accurate and orderly account of his life that included the names of some of the religious and civil leaders of that day (Luke 1:1–5; 2:1–3; 3:1–3). Jesus Christ is as much a part of history as Caesar, Herod, and Pilate.

The incarnation of Christ assures us that God cared enough for sinners to enter into our world and experience our joys and sorrows, temptations and trials, needs and burdens, suffering and pain, and even to bear our sins on the cross (1 Peter 2:24). The Christ of yesterday is seen in the gospel records as the loving Friend who converses at the dinner table, attends weddings, weeps with mourners, plays with children, feeds the hungry, and welcomes the rejects. But he hasn't changed! He's the same today! We should never tire of hearing about Jesus or preaching about Jesus.

Today

He is the Christ of personal experience. We don't preach Christ as though he were only one of many departed actors who once walked the stage of history. Unlike other members of the cast mentioned in Scripture, Jesus Christ is alive today and is actively at work building his church. As Lord of history, he wrote the script; and as Mediator and High Priest, he is directing the entire production from his throne at the Father's right hand in heaven. According to Philippians 3:10, we may not only know him as an historic person, but we can experience "the power of his resurrection and the fellowship of his sufferings" in our daily lives.

"Christ died" is simply a fact of history. "Christ died for our sins" is the theological interpretation of that fact (1 Cor. 15:3). "He loved me and gave himself for me" (Gal. 2:20) is the personal and saving application of that truth, made possible because Jesus Christ is alive and "able to save completely those who come to God through him" (Heb. 7:25). Most believers can tell you what Jesus Christ did when he was here on earth, but they have a difficult time explaining what he is doing now in heaven. *Savior, Lord,* and *Teacher* are familiar titles, but *Advocate, High Priest,* and *Mediator* don't seem to be as meaningful.[2] The Christ of yesterday was at least a flesh and blood person who went places and did things, but what's so important about the Christ of today who is sitting on a throne in heaven? That's the theme of the Epistle to the Hebrews and it's a message desperately needed by God's people today.

Jesus Christ is still caring for people just as we're told in the Gospels written by Matthew, Mark, Luke, and John. But as the risen, glorified Lord, he has ascended to heaven, sent the Holy Spirit, and is no longer limited to one time and one place. He is the Christ of today for all believers, no matter where they live; his eyes are on them and his ears are open to their cries. We can always come to his throne of grace and by faith receive from him all the help we need (Heb. 4:14–16).

Forever

He is the Christ of prophecy. Jesus Christ is the major theme of prophecy in both the Old and the New Testaments. The Old Testament prophets announced, "He is coming!" and the New Testament apostles assure us, "He is coming again!" The church of the first century lived on tiptoe as they awaited his promised return, but too many preachers today dismiss the prophetic message as mere speculation rather than biblical revelation and so they leave it to the cults to preach prophecy. There was a time when God's people were interested in and excited by the truths of biblical prophecy, even to the point of holding great conventions to consider the truth of the return of Jesus Christ. Unfortunately many prophetic teachers failed to connect prophecy with practical Christian living, and gradually heaven became a comfortable future destination rather than a compelling present motivation.

And yet there is great value in preaching biblical prophecy, provided we give our messages the kind of practical emphasis that is found in Scripture. Consider Paul's first letter to the Thessalonians as an example. The apostle presents the expectation of our Lord's return as an evidence of salvation (1:9–10) as well as a motivation for evangelism (2:17–20), Christian growth (3:11–13), comfort (4:13–18), and godly living (5:23–24; see 1 John 3:1–3). John didn't write the Book of the Revelation so that scholars could draw charts but so that Christians going through persecution could draw strength from the assurance of Christ's promised victory.

Preaching Christ Is What the Preacher Needs

Preaching Christ not only helps the listener, but it also helps the preacher! For one thing, preaching Christ keeps us from preaching ourselves or using the pulpit to display our abilities. "No man can bear witness to Christ and to himself at the same time," said Professor James Denney. "No man can give the impression that he himself is clever and that Christ is mighty to save."[3] Preaching Christ means preaching to *express* and not to *impress*. Our example is John the Baptist who pointed to Jesus, the Lamb of God, and refused to talk about himself (John 1:19–29). Jesus is the Word, but

John was only the voice (v. 23), and you can't see a voice. Jesus is the Bridegroom, while John is but the best man (3:27–30). Jesus is the Light, but John was only the humble clay lamp that carried the light to others (5:35). John's desire ought to be the desire of every preacher of the Word, "He must become greater; I must become less" (3:30).

Preaching Christ also enables us to preach the whole Bible. "All Scripture is God-breathed and is useful" (2 Tim. 3:16), and we're commanded to live by "every word" God has given us (Matt. 4:4). This means that we must give our people a balanced spiritual diet and not just linger in those portions of the Bible that we enjoy preaching the most (or that preach the easiest). Christ is found in all the Scriptures if only we have eyes to see; and when people see Christ, the Spirit enables them to fulfill what the Scriptures tell them to do.

Preaching Christ encourages the minister to preach in the present tense. One of the complaints of the people in the pews is that too many ministers preach in the past tense and never find (as Phillips Brooks put it) the place where truth touches everyday life.[4] Abstract truth may excite the lone philosopher in your congregation, but it will never change the life of the average worshiper. Every attribute of God and every Christian virtue is embodied in Jesus Christ who is the supreme example of holy balanced living.

Furthermore, the basic doctrines of the Christian faith are all embodied in Christ "who has become for us wisdom from God—that is, our righteousness, holiness and redemption" (1 Cor. 1:30). Ignore Jesus Christ and you can't teach Christian doctrine. Some years ago I was struggling through a book on the history of the Victorian Age in England when I happened on a new biography of Queen Victoria. I switched to the biography and had a delightful time learning about both the queen and Victorian England. So it is with Christ: When we focus on him, the doctrines of Scripture are easier to understand and apply in our daily lives.

Finally, and most important, when we preach Christ, we can be sure of the help of the Holy Spirit, for he was sent to glorify the Son of God (John 16:12–15). No amount of talent, experience, or homiletical skill can impart power to the pulpit, because effective witness to Christ comes only from the power of the Spirit (Acts 1:8). As I noted in the last chapter, we want the gospel to come to people "not simply with words, but also with power, with the Holy Spirit and with deep conviction" (1 Thess. 1:5). For that to happen, we must preach Christ.

How to Preach Christ

You don't preach Christ by completing your sermon outline and then asking yourself, *Where can I fit Jesus into this message?* The truth about Jesus isn't a condiment you sprinkle on the meal after it's been prepared. Jesus Christ is the "main course" around which everything else is arranged. The inspired writers of Scripture connected both doctrine and duty to Jesus Christ, and we must follow their example.

"Be kind and compassionate to one another, forgiving each other" is the kind of wise counsel that almost any mature person could give, but the preacher must add "just as in Christ God forgave you" (Eph. 4:32). Forgiveness must be connected with Jesus Christ and the forgiveness we've experienced through him. An unbelieving marriage counselor could exhort a husband to love his wife, but the Christian counselor adds "just as Christ loved the church and gave himself up for her" (Eph. 5:25). "We love because he first loved us" (1 John 4:19). When Paul wanted to encourage the negligent Corinthian believers to contribute to the fund for the Jerusalem saints, he connected their giving with what their Savior had done for them. "For you know the grace of our Lord Jesus Christ, that though he was rich, yet for your sakes he became poor, so that you through his poverty might become rich" (2 Cor. 8:9).

Moses followed a similar approach when he taught God's Law to the new generation of Israelites preparing to enter the Promised Land. The word *remember* is used fourteen times in Deuteronomy and the word *forget* at least nine times. If they remembered what the Lord had done for them, they would have no problem hearing his Word and obeying it. Why should they keep the Sabbath? "Remember that you were slaves in Egypt and that the LORD your God brought you out of there with a mighty hand and an outstretched arm" (Deut. 5:15). Why should they be generous to their servants? "Remember that you were slaves in Egypt and the LORD your God redeemed you" (15:15). Why should they take care of the aliens and strangers in the land? "Remember that you were slaves in Egypt" (24:18). What God has done for his people should determine what his people do for him and for others.

Once we accept this biblical principle, we must permit it to control our lives and the work that we do. This means cultivating a close relationship with Jesus Christ so that our devotion to him gives us open eyes to see him in Scripture, a willing heart to obey him, and a ready tongue to proclaim him to others. Preaching Christ isn't a homiletical rule we slavishly obey or a gimmick that we turn on and off as the occasion demands. Preaching Christ is a spiritual intuition that should always be at work in our lives. It's the result of spending disciplined time with Christ in the Word, worshiping him, praying, and seeking to please him in all that we do. If our hearts are to be stirred and our tongues are to become God's instruments to proclaim Christ to others, then we must constantly see Jesus in his beauty and victory as did the sons of Korah in Psalm 45. The more our people see Christ in the Word and in our lives, the more they will love him; and the more they love him, the more they will obey him and do his will; and that's what preaching Christ is all about.

"The best sermons are the sermons which are fullest of Christ," said Charles Spurgeon. "A sermon without Christ is an awful, a horrible thing. It is an empty well; it is a cloud without rain; it is a tree twice dead, plucked up by the roots."[5]

Four
We Preach to Real People

Stay in touch with real people. . . . Jesus did. You should too.

Bob Briner
The Management Methods of Jesus

When you're listening to a sermon, it doesn't take long to discover whether the preacher is speaking "to the air" or speaking personally to the hearts of individuals. I once heard a scholarly but remote message that was obviously the next chapter of a book the preacher was writing. Five minutes after the benediction, I couldn't have told you what he said, but I could tell you that it never reached my heart. That was unusual because I'm a very attentive and sympathetic listener when it comes to sermons.

If a preacher takes thirty minutes to deliver a sermon to two hundred worshipers, he uses up one hundred valuable hours, plus whatever time he spent preparing the sermon. Collectively, that's a great deal of time for people to give up without getting something helpful in return. Henry David Thoreau wouldn't have called himself an evangelical believer, but he was right on target when he wrote, "As if you could kill time without injuring eternity."[1] We do both when we fail to preach to real people.

In seventeenth-century England, condemned prisoners were given the privilege of hearing a "condemnation sermon on repentance" to help prepare them for death. On one occasion the chaplain of the jail, Mr. Swinton, used a sermon he had preached at the university. Slavishly following his manuscript, he concluded by saying he would give the remainder of the message on the next Lord's Day. Unfortunately his captive congregation never got to hear the rest of the sermon because they were taken out the next day and hanged. Mr. Swinton obviously wasn't preaching to real people.[2]

Think in Terms of Individuals and Not Assemblies

We know that we are preaching to real people when we think in terms of individuals and not assemblies. In contrast to the story about Mr. Swinton, consider the account of what happened when a mother took her young daughter to hear Charles Spurgeon preach. After listening for about fifteen minutes, the girl whispered to her mother, "Mother, is Mr. Spurgeon speaking to *me*?" Yes, he was speaking to her, as well as to the five thousand other individuals seated in the sanctuary. Spurgeon attracted huge crowds but he preached to individuals.

From April 30, 1945, to April 30, 1972, *Arthur Godfrey Time* was the reigning daytime radio program on CBS with more than forty million listeners a week hanging on to Godfrey's every word, including the commercials. When asked the secret of his success as a "radio voice," Godfrey explained that he didn't envision himself speaking to crowds of people living in that mysterious place called "Radioland." Rather, he saw himself as a friend chatting with one individual—a man driving a truck, a woman doing the dishes, a patient lying in a hospital bed, perhaps a lonely man or woman with nothing to do and nobody to care. Everything about his presentation said to the listener, "I'm interested in you and have something important to share."[3]

It's a red-letter day in your life when you discover that congregations really don't do anything except assemble. In the local church, *individuals* get the work done, so the smart minister preaches to individuals. That doesn't mean that we single people out and address them pontifically from the pulpit. But it does mean that we adopt an approach in our delivery that says to the people: Yes, I know I'm on this platform and occasionally behind this pulpit, and you're sitting down there. But that's only so you can all see me and hear me. I'd much rather be sitting with you and sharing this message. I can't do that, so I'll do the next best thing and deliver my message as if I were at your side.

Jesus was usually surrounded by crowds, but he always had time for individuals and never put them on hold. After preaching the Sermon on the Mount, our Lord took time to meet the needs of a paralyzed servant boy. While on the way to the house of Jairus, he stopped to help a poor woman who had been afflicted for twelve years. Peter saw three thousand people converted on the Day of Pentecost, but he took time to minister to one beggar at the temple gate, and two thousand more people trusted Christ. We win the world and we change situations one person at a time.

Respect Individuals as Persons Created in the Image of God

Real people have minds to think with and don't appreciate condescending sermons that elevate the preacher and belittle the listener. Jesus never talked down to people. He had the gift of starting where they were and making profound things simple and simple things profound. He encouraged people to think. Real people also have a heart to feel with, and Jesus respected those feelings. As he welcomed tax collectors and other social and religious outcasts, he shared his love with them while at the same time honestly probing their hearts and meeting their deepest needs. He neither ignored nor exploited their feelings.

Real people have a will to decide with, but Jesus never tricked anybody or forced anyone into making decisions. His lament was "how often I have longed to gather your children together, as a hen gathers her chicks under her wings, but you were not willing!" (Luke 13:34). Paul followed his example: "For the appeal we make does not spring from error or impure motives, nor are we trying to trick you" (1 Thess. 2:3).[4] Most of the itinerant teachers in Paul's day used mental gymnastics to astonish and manipulate their listeners, but Paul spoke clearly and sincerely (2 Cor. 4:1–2).

The difficulty today is that we minister in a world where the technology, values, and philosophies of society combine to dehumanize people.[5] "If you want a picture of the future," wrote George Orwell in *Nineteen Eighty-Four*, "imagine a boot stamping on a human face—for ever."[6] Lose your face and you've lost your identity. You become what Orwell called "an un-person."

The goal of our ministry is to "present everyone per-fect in Christ" (Col. 1:28), and you don't do that by dehumanizing people. The more people become like Christ, the more they become their true selves and their best selves. Jesus doesn't destroy individuality or identity. He didn't melt the twelve apostles together and manufacture a group of bland faceless followers. Each man was unique, yet each one was like Jesus. Christlike individuality is one of the important differ-ences between Christians and cultists.

Speak the Truth in Love

Another way we treat people as humans and not things is when we speak the truth in love, but it deserves special attention. *What* we say in our sermons is important, but so is *how we say it.* That's why Paul wrote about "speaking the truth in love" (Eph. 4:15). More than one ethical teacher has reminded us that truth without love can become brutality, but love with-out truth can become hypocrisy, and we don't want either one.

Certainly there's a place for righteous anger, but it must be mixed with love and become anguish or we will destroy people, "for man's anger does not bring about the righteous life that God desires" (James 1:20). The Anglican evangelist John Berridge recommended to ministers that they "begin with ripping up the audi-ence, and Moses will lend you a carving knife." Charles Simeon followed that advice for a time; but then he saw the folly of "preachers who act like butchers." His own seasoned counsel was, "Let your preaching come from the heart. Love should be the spring of all actions and especially of a minister's. If a man's heart be full of love, he will rarely offend."[7]

Preach to Meet
Universal Human Needs

Henri Nouwen made a luminous statement when he wrote, "Ultimately, I believe that what is most personal is also the most universal."[8] In other words, when we're preaching about universal needs, we're also ministering to people personally and touching them where they hurt. Obscure texts or trendy topics don't allure the wise preacher nor do they strengthen the discouraged believer. When the apostle John wrote his Gospel for the whole world, he majored on the universal images: light and darkness, birth, hunger and thirst, the wind and the harvest, to name a few. He also dealt with universal human emotions: faith and doubt, love and hate, fear and confidence, sorrow and joy, and suffering.

"Read diligently the great book of mankind," Samuel Johnson advised his young friend James Boswell, who was leaving England to study law in Holland.[9] That's wise counsel for the pastor as well as for the lawyer, for if we don't know our people, we'll have a difficult time helping them come to know God. There's a close connection between loving God's people and knowing God better (1 John 4:7–8). While serving as interim minister at a church in Dummer, George Whitefield wrote in his journal, "I frequently learnt as much by an afternoon's visit, as in a week's study."[10] I can identify with that experience and thank God for it.

For some reason, many ministers have the absurd idea that they must choose between being effective preachers or caring pastors, as if there were two callings to ministry instead of one. Let Phillips Brooks answer the matter: "The preacher needs to be pastor, that he may preach to real men. The pastor needs to be preacher, that he may keep the dignity of his work alive. The preacher who is not a pastor grows remote. The pastor who is not a preacher grows petty."[11] In other words, the preacher must be a pastor to have sympathy and the pastor must be a preacher to have authority.

Faithful ministers who devote themselves to one congregation for many years can bear witness that the size of the church has no bearing on the breadth of their vision or the extent of their opportunity. Every local church is a microcosm of humanity and the well of human nature is deep. "I have traveled a good deal in Concord," wrote Thoreau,[12] and by knowing one place and people well, he came to know all places and people and wrote skillfully about them. W. Robertson Nicoll said that the first qualification for a good journalist was "interestedness," and I would say the same thing about a good preacher. "Now the born journalist is interested by everything," wrote Nicoll. "Humanity concerns him."[13]

Charles Schulz has his *Peanuts* character Linus expressing what many preachers must feel: "I love humanity. It's people I can't stand!" But like it or not, people are what ministry is all about; and the sooner we learn to love the sheep and the lambs, the easier it will be to feed them and lead them (John 21:15–17). But we can't love people at a distance and still be faithful shepherds. Paradoxical as it sounds, when we get to know *our own* flock, we are better prepared to minister to *any* flock, because people are people and their needs are universal.

Prepare Your Messages with Your People in Mind

Don't pastors always think of their people when preparing a message? you may ask. Aren't we preaching the Word to encourage and help our people? Well, that's what we're supposed to do, but unless we have a shepherd's heart, we may be so interested in *content* that we ignore *intent.* I don't agree with Harry Emerson Fosdick's theology, but his approach to preaching was wise and practical. "A lecture is chiefly concerned with a subject to be elucidated," he wrote; "a sermon is chiefly concerned with an object to be achieved."[14] In short, our purpose is to achieve an object by explaining and applying a portion of the Bible. If you're called by God, then you're to be both pastor and teacher (Eph. 4:11), because the shepherd (pastor) leads and feeds the flock by means of the Word of God.

A very fine congregation once invited me to become their preaching pastor, assuring me that all I had to do was preach. I wouldn't be required to visit the people, do any counseling, conduct weddings or funerals, or even attend board meetings. When I graciously refused their invitation, the committee was shocked; and when I explained why, they were shocked even more. I said, "You're asking me to minister to a faceless crowd and I can't do it. Sure, I could preach acceptable sermons week by week, but they wouldn't be messages that would meet the needs of the people. I'd be distanced from the church family and that would make the sermons less and less personal and more and more academic. It won't work."

In large churches where senior pastors preach to people by the acre, they've learned to keep their hearts warm and tender by ministering to as many individuals as possible. It isn't easy but it can be done.

John Henry Jowett gave a helpful piece of advice when he said:

> I keep in the circle of my mind at least a dozen
> men and women, very varied in their natural tem-

peraments, and very dissimilar in their daily circumstances. These are not mere abstractions. . . . These are real men and women whom I know. . . . When I am preparing my work, my mind is constantly glancing round this invisible circle, and I consider how I can so serve the bread of this particular truth as to provide nutriment for all.

Then he added, "Gentlemen, our messages must be related to life, to lives, and we must make everybody feel that our key fits the lock of his own private door."[15]

Another aspect of visualizing our people as we prepare the message is *anticipating objections and difficulties.* Some people's minds are like medieval fortresses, with their fears and prejudices united to prevent God's truth from getting in. (Paul may have had some of these people in mind when he wrote 2 Corinthians 10:1–6.) Whether they know it or not, everybody in the congregation has some worldview that helps to stabilize and guide their lives. Our task is to help make that worldview more biblical, so we have to meet their objections and answer their arguments. When a preacher says, "Now at this point, some of you may be thinking . . ." it is a gentle but powerful way to open the gates, lower the drawbridge, and let the truth march in and take command.

Be Sensitive to the Power of Words

Never underestimate the power of words, either spoken or printed. According to Norman Cousins, for every word in Adolf Hitler's *Mein Kampf,* 125 people lost their lives in World War 2.[16] "Death and life are in the power of the tongue" (Prov. 18:21 NASB), and wise is the preacher who uses the power of speech to the glory of God. The tongue can destroy like a fire or a dangerous beast (James 3:5–8); it can be hurtful and lethal "like a club or a sword or a sharp arrow" (Prov. 25:18). But the tongue can also bring healing like honey (16:24) or refreshment like cold water (25:25). The right words can encourage the depressed (12:25) and strengthen the weary (Isa. 50:4). The wrong words can send people home from the meeting carrying more burdens than when they came.

I'm not suggesting that preachers subscribe to *Politically Correct Digest* and tiptoe through the sermon lest they offend somebody. If we're faithful to the gospel, we can't escape the offense of the cross (Gal. 5:11), but let's do our best not to deliberately offend people from the pulpit. "In your teaching show integrity, seriousness and soundness of speech that cannot be condemned" (Titus 2:7–8).

A good friend once introduced me at a conference by saying, "Watch out! This man's sense of humor is lethal!" He had seen me get a congregation smiling or even laughing and then, when they least expected it, hit home with a spiritual truth that they might have ducked had they not been diverted. There's a place for wit and humor in the pulpit,[17] but there's no room there for a stand-up comic or a show-off. We want to send the congregation home awed by the greatness of God, not laughing at the cleverness of the preacher.

Since what we say with the tongue comes from the heart, we had better be careful about the vocabulary we use when we talk to ourselves. When we least expect it, what we've been saying in our hearts will come out of our lips and embarrass us. "Above all else, guard your heart, for it is the wellspring of life" (Prov. 4:23). Let's take care not to muddy the waters.

Finally, it's a dangerous thing to use slang in an attempt to give the impression that we're in tune with the contemporary scene. To call the twelve apostles "those guys who followed Jesus" is vulgar if not irreverent. Every vocation has its jargon that serves as a helpful shortcut on the job, but it probably should stay out of the pulpit; and crude street language has no place in a sermon. I once heard an internationally known preacher swear in a seminary chapel pulpit and then ask the president, "Is this being broadcast?" Granted, the preacher was quoting another man, but he could have handled it better.

If the sword of the Spirit pierces a listener's heart, that's one thing, because God's Word is a two-edged sword that brings healing as well as cutting. But if we stab people deliberately with words that hurt but don't heal, we're abusing the great gift of language as well as the hearts and minds of people God loves and for whom Jesus died.

Preach with Eternity in Mind

It's true that "[God] richly provides us with everything for our enjoyment" (1 Tim. 6:17), but it's also true that life has its share of trouble and sorrow and passes quickly away (Ps. 90:10). Sooner than we expect, the night comes and our work is done (John 9:4). You and I don't know when we'll preach our last sermon or when a worshiper will hear his or her last sermon, so we'd better examine what we do in the light of eternity. Jonathan Edwards frequently asked himself, "How much shall I value this upon my deathbed?" Joyless? Morose? Not at all. Moses prayed, "Teach us to number our days aright, that we may gain a heart of wisdom" (Ps. 90:12).

We Preach
to Be Understood

Five

I design plain truth for plain people.

John Wesley

While on a layover at the Salt Lake City airport, I began
to pass the time by chatting with the captain of our flight.
I soon discovered that he was unhappy because the air
traffic controllers were threatening to go on strike.

"Your contact with them is mainly by radio," I said.
"Do you ever get to know them personally?"

He smiled. "You get to know them fairly well just by
the way they give you directions for landing. Most controllers just give the instructions clearly and concisely,
but there's a lady controller at a California airport who
reads to us right from the operations manual! One
pilot I know listened to her for several minutes, and
when she asked him if he understood, he replied,
'Ma'am, you sounded so much like my wife, I didn't
hear a word you said!'"

Later, as our plane flew to Los Angeles, I pondered
that pilot's answer. I asked myself, *When I preach, do peo-*

ple hear only instructions from an operations manual or do they hear the living God speaking to them through his Word? Or perhaps they hear a different voice that distracts them from hearing God's voice and they totally miss the message. Sobering thoughts.

When we prepare a message, we must keep in mind the elements that are involved:

- Understanding the text[1]
- Determining the object of the message
- Stating that object clearly
- Planning the development of the message in light of that object
- Deciding how to get the people's attention and hold their interest

Understanding the Text

According to our Lord's parable of the sower, unless people understand the Word of God, they can't receive it into their hearts where it can take root and bear fruit (Matt. 13:1–9, 18–23).[2] In the parable Jesus explained that the hearers with hard hearts can't receive the Word because they don't understand it, so Satan snatches the seed away. *A humble prepared heart is essential to an understanding of God's truth.* "If anyone chooses to do God's will, he will find out whether my teaching comes from God or whether I speak on my own" (John 7:17). F. W. Robertson called obedience "the organ of spiritual knowledge."[3]

The listeners in the parable with the shallow hearts and the crowded hearts also failed to understand the message. The shallow-hearted group expected only joy from following Christ and gave no thought to suffering. When persecution came, it exposed their insincere faith. The people with the crowded hearts didn't understand the message because they failed to pull the "weeds" out of their hearts (repentance) so that the good seed would have room to grow. It was the people who heard the Word *and understood it* who received the good seed, cultivated it, and produced fruit.

Working Hard

If we are to succeed in explaining and applying the text to people in the congregation, we must understand the text ourselves and apply it to our own lives. This means investing hours of hard work, week after week, reading and studying the Scriptures, meditating, praying, and serving our Lord and our people. You know what time of day (or night) is best for you to do creative work, so set it aside, guard it, and make good use of it. Don't complain about the time you don't have; prioritize wisely the time you do have.

Ministers who complain that they don't have enough time for study (and who does?) should remember that *the conscientious preacher who is in the will of God is always preparing.* Ministry isn't a series of activities that we turn on and off like the computer. We don't just "do ministry"; we *are* ministers, and therefore we can't escape ministering. We can meditate on a text while driving down the highway; we can read a book while waiting in the dentist's office; we can get a fresh illustration while standing in line at the supermarket checkout counter. Life is ministry and ministry is life, and we must not separate what God has put together.

There are days when we can hardly wait to get to the desk, open the Bible, and start working on the message. We feel like a cook preparing a banquet or a tour guide plotting an exciting journey. But there are also days when we feel more like a general making a battle plan or a miner crawling through a tunnel. No matter what our feelings, we can still get into the text and let the text get into us. Studying that is motivated only by how we feel can't produce authentic biblical preaching. After all, the people who originally penned the Scriptures didn't always feel healthy and happy, and perhaps we'll understand their messages better if we suffer a bit.

Looking Ahead

One of the advantages of planned preaching is the opportunity you have to work ahead. You get a set of file folders (or you open files in your computer), label each folder with a message topic and text, and each time you get an idea, add it to the file. The fact that you plan your texts and themes in advance doesn't mean the Lord can't break in and give you a prophetic word for that hour based on a different text. In fact the interruption will call attention to the importance of the message. However, if more and more of your sermons are "interruptions," it's likely that series preaching isn't your greatest strength. Don't apologize; some of the church's most effective preachers rarely preached series of sermons or expositions of entire books. They delivered the messages God gave them week by week. This is a much more difficult approach, but you must be true to your gifts and calling as they were to theirs.

There's a danger, however, that we plan so far ahead that the sermons become isolated lectures totally divorced from the preacher's life and the life of the church. I've heard of ministers who have a full year's ministry all blocked out, with embalmed outlines buried in their files and waiting to be resurrected and preached. But the archaeologist who *fails to breathe new life into the message* will not have a congregation that hears the Lord speaking exciting new truths or sees him work in fresh ways. In my conference ministry, I've preached some sermons thirty times, but each time I invested many hours asking God to preach it to me in refreshing new ways lest I find myself a tour guide in a biblical museum.

Study Habits

I like to keep my basic tools around me so I can lay hands on them before I forget what I'm investigating in the text. If I'm expounding a book, I keep the best commentaries near me on the desk and don't put them back on the library shelf until the series has been completed. It isn't necessary to consult twenty or thirty commentaries as you exegete a text. Learn what the best commentaries are and use the ones that help you most. Books are tools, and just as tools must match the strength and skill of the workman, so books must be suited to the student. If you find that a "classic" commentary encumbers you instead of enlightens you, don't feel guilty. Just lay it aside and give yourself time to "grow into it." The book may be whispering to you, "I have much more to say to you, more than you can now bear" (John 16:12). One of the blessed by-products of ministry is the constant opportunity for growth.

Is it necessary to make your own translation of the passage you're studying? I'm a heretic in this matter and reply: not necessarily. But you ought to study carefully the key words and the textual matters that relate to interpretation. So many excellent translations and language helps are available today that even the average student can mine a great deal of gold from the text. If doing your own translation delights you and doesn't consume time that might better be invested elsewhere, then by all means enjoy yourself. But I'm prone to agree with Ralph Waldo Emerson who admitted that he preferred reading accurate translations of the classics to reading the originals. Why swim the river when somebody has already built a sound bridge?[4]

So read the text in several translations and paraphrases, check the original languages, do some serious thinking, and let the Scriptures minister to your own heart. Don't read homiletical commentaries and sermons on the passage until you've developed your own approach. If you get ideas from other preachers' sermons, document them and give credit when you quote. If they've quoted somebody else, try to get back to the original and be sure the quotation is accurate.[5] The temptation to plagiarize is a great one, especially when you're under pressure. I've told students that in my sermon preparation, I milk a lot of cows but I make my own butter; and if I pour some cream out of other people's pails, I give them credit.

Determining the Object of the Message

While you're engaged in reading and studying, keep asking yourself and the Lord, *What's the major message of this passage?* Don't search for obscure themes; stick to the main road and leave the detours to the homiletical Athenians who are always looking for something new. Life is too short for us to preach all the great themes in Scripture, so don't waste time pursuing minor matters. Here are some hints for determining that overriding theme:

- Look for "boundary verses" that seem to mark out thematic boundaries, such as John 14:1 and 27 ("Do not let your hearts be troubled") and 2 Corinthians 4:1 and 16 ("we do not lose heart").
- Watch for repeated words and phrases, such as "Why are you downcast, O my soul?" in Psalms 42–43, "fear" in Isaiah 41, "better" in Hebrews, and "mourn" in Revelation 18. Check your Greek and Hebrew concordances.
- Be alert to the images in the passage. The image of the flock dominates John 10 and relates to chapter 9, which is the account of a "sheep" who was thrown out by the religious leaders but taken in by the Good Shepherd. In James 3 you find six pictures of the tongue illustrating the right and wrong use of speech. Isaiah 59 paints several graphic pictures of a corrupt society, including a traffic jam (v. 14)!
- Be sensitive to the "atmosphere" of the text and don't approach poetry the way you would approach narrative or theological arguments. Galatians 1 and 2 are clearly autobiographical and describe Paul's defense of his message and his ministry, while Galatians 3 and 4 are theological and constitute Paul's argument for salvation by grace alone. We read 1 Corinthians 13 at weddings (and sometimes at funerals), but Paul wrote it to be read at local church business meetings! We also read Psalm 23 at funerals, and surely it fits (v. 4), but the psalm speaks about God's care "all the days of my life" (v. 6), not just when I die.
- Note the way New Testament writers use Old Testament verses, images, and allusions. The background for John 10 is surely Ezekiel 34 plus Psalms 23 and 100. Habakkuk 2:4 is quoted in Romans

The Dynamics of Preaching

1:17; Galatians 3:11; and Hebrews 10:37–38, each time emphasizing a different aspect of justification by faith.

- Note also the way the authors of the Epistles refer to experiences recorded in the four Gospels. Peter has a number of these allusions in his two letters. Give yourself time. Immerse yourself in the text and apply it to your own heart. Trust your gut-level feelings to point you in the right direction. Prayer, meditation, and honesty will carry you through.

A final suggestion: As you exegete the passage and take notes, use small pieces of paper (3 x 4 inches) and write only one idea on each piece, giving each one a thematic title (for example, "unbelief") and the Scripture verse in the passage to which it belongs. When your spadework is done and you've moved into developing an outline, you can arrange the notes on your desk and put them where they belong. Many you will use, some you will file away for future use, and some will end up in the wastebasket.[6] This is much more efficient than taking notes on a legal pad and then having to separate them and decide where to put them. Using smaller pieces of notepaper gives you much more flexibility.

Stating the Object of the Message Clearly and Concisely

Those who teach preaching and write about preaching use different names for an important element in the sermon—stating the object clearly and concisely. Following the lead of Austin Phelps in his book *Theory of Preaching,* Charles Koller and Lloyd Perry christened the important sentence that states the object "the propositional statement."[7] Haddon Robinson writes of "the big idea."[8] John Henry Jowett maintained that no sermon was ready for preaching "until we can express its theme in a short, pregnant sentence as clear as crystal."[9] Call it what you will, this sentence is the heart and soul of the message. Perhaps a definition would help: *The proposition is the statement of a timeless truth found in Scripture. It is in the present tense. It declares the intent and determines the content of the sermon.* And perhaps some examples will help:

> The Holy Spirit enables Christians to witness successfully (Acts 1:8).
>
> The purpose of prayer is to glorify God (Matt. 6:9).
>
> Just think of the joys of a life that God blesses! (Matt. 5:1–12).
>
> The fact that we're going to heaven someday ought to make a difference in our lives every day (John 17:24).
>
> We may forget our decisions, but our decisions won't forget us (Gal. 6:6–10).
>
> It's a dangerous thing to pray out of the will of God (Matt. 20:20–28).

The proposition or purpose statement unifies the *content* of the sermon, so it discourages the preacher from covering too much territory or wandering off into foreign lands. It also clarifies the *intent* of the sermon so the listeners know where the message is going. No sermon can include everything that's taught in the text, although some of the Puritans came close to accomplishing this difficult feat. The proposition helps us focus our studies wisely and select our materials carefully. Just as a river without banks becomes a swamp, so a sermon without a clear proposition becomes a rambling religious speech that tries to say so much it ends up saying nothing. Asked about an address he heard Emerson give, James Russell Lowell said, "It began nowhere and ended everywhere."[10] Perhaps Emerson needed a propositional statement.

In his seminal book *Design for Preaching,* H. Grady Davis reminds us that a generalization (which is what a proposition is) "condenses a broad area of experience into a single statement, and sees a large truth in a single glance." Then he adds, "For it is the generalizations that organize the material."[11] Those statements should be read again and pondered.

The proposition isn't a statement about the sermon; it's a statement about God and human life. It must be specific enough for the listeners to get their hands on it, interesting enough for them to want to stay with it, and so full of life and anticipation that they can't let go of it. It touches people where they live and when expanded in the sermon, it makes people see, think, feel, and want to obey. Refining the purpose statement is a difficult task but a most important one. At least three factors are involved in the development of the proposition: (1) the truth found in the text, (2) the needs of the church, and (3) the constraint in our own hearts. We aren't just giving a lecture about a portion of Scripture; we're seeking to meet the needs of a church family collectively and of family members individually. Any preacher can make a tolerable outline of almost any passage and preach from it, but that would be "sermonizing" and not real exposition of the Word of God. Unfortunately, an outline isn't a message any more than a recipe is a meal or a blueprint is a house, so be sure that the propositional statement is connected to life as well as truth.

So as you study the text, take time to study your people and your own heart, and ask the Spirit to bring these elements together so you can give expression to a proposition that will express the truth of the text. This can lead to a sermon that will meet the needs of the people. If you've done your homework in the study and your pastoral work with the people, the Spirit has something tangible to work with and won't disappoint you.

Developing the Message Outline

The development of the message grows out of the union of the text and the proposition. If the proposition is what it ought to be, it will contain the "homiletical DNA" that will determine how the message develops. Let's consider a familiar passage, 1 John 1:5–10:

> This is the message we have heard from him and declare to you: God is light; in him there is no darkness at all. If we claim to have fellowship with him yet walk in the darkness, we lie and do not live by the truth. But if we walk in the light, as he is in the light, we have fellowship with one another, and the blood of Jesus, his Son, purifies us from all sin. If we claim to be without sin, we deceive ourselves and the truth is not in us. If we confess our sins, he is faithful and just and will forgive us our sins and purify us from all unrighteousness. If we claim we have not sinned, we

make him out to be a liar and his word has no place in our lives.

Even a cursory reading of the passage reveals that there are three *deceptions* God's people must avoid if they want to be in fellowship with God:

1. Trying to deceive others (v. 6)
2. Trying to deceive ourselves (v. 8)
3. Trying to deceive God (v. 10)

If that approach seems a bit negative, take it from the positive viewpoint: If we would cultivate Christian character and fellowship with God, there are four *conditions* we must meet:

1. We must recognize that God is holy (v. 5)
2. We must be honest with God's people (vv. 6–7)
3. We must be honest with ourselves (v. 8)
4. We must be honest with God (vv. 9–10)

The words in italics are what we call "key words." They describe each of the main points in the development of the message. In the first outline, each point is a form of deception; in the second, each point is a condition we must meet. The points are parallel and belong together. It's an approach that enables people to follow the message and understand the text and apply it. When you change the key word, you change the approach of the message. For example, the proposition might be: When we start living as though our God is not a holy God, we've taken the first step toward ruin. John describes the *stages* in this sad experience:

1. We begin to lie to others (v. 6)
2. We begin to lie to ourselves (v. 8)
3. We try to lie to God (v. 10)

John also points out that in each of these stages, the believer incurs some fearful *losses:*

1. The truth no longer controls us (v. 6)
2. The truth is no longer within us (v. 8)
3. The truth is no longer welcome within us (v. 10)

If you change the intent of the proposition, you will probably have to change the key word as well. Remember, the key word is always a noun and always plural. Because it characterizes the main points of the message, the key word must be concrete, precise, and accurate. Although Paul uses the word *things* frequently (see Romans 8 and Philippians 3), it isn't a good key word for today's preacher because it's too broad. A proposition such as "Paul tells us several things about prayer" isn't likely to attract much interest. "If you decide to be a person of prayer, it will radically change your life" is much more incisive. Your key word could be *ways* or *changes* or *alterations.*

Another key word that needs to be used with care is *reasons,* not because it isn't a good word, but because it announces to the congregation, "I'm going to debate with you, so get ready!" Halford Luccock used to remind his Yale Divinity School students, "People don't come to church to hear reasons; they come to see visions."

You ought to own a good thesaurus and a book of synonyms, but your best tool will be a dependable dictionary of synonyms that gives you definitions of the words and illustrates the fine shades of meaning that distinguish them.[12] For example, there's a difference between *results* and *consequences.* The words shouldn't be used interchangeably. Mark Twain said that the difference between the right word and the almost right word was the difference between lightning and the lightning bug. The wise preacher will seek to be a student of words and use them as jewelers handle precious gems or surgeons their instruments. Most good dictionaries list synonyms and antonyms, and the preacher will want to own and use the best linguistic tools. It's important to know the value of the words we use and to treat them with respect.

The propositional approach to preaching makes for clear outlines, but if we aren't careful, it can lead to mechanical sermon preparation that results in messages that are predictable. The beginning preacher, like the beginning musician, must obey the rules and learn the basics. You don't break the rules until the rules have first broken you. But the proposition doesn't always have to be an affirmation (Jesus wants to increase our faith). It can be a question (Whatever else our churches may be known for today, are they known for their great faith?) or even an exclamation (Think of what could happen to our families, our community, and this church if we really exercised faith in God!). There's even a place for the hortatory proposition (Keep on praying!). Study and experience will help the minister develop the kind of intuition needed for framing the proposition.

Getting and Holding Attention

We have three goals in mind as we introduce the sermon: getting our listeners' attention, telling them what the sermon is to be about, and convincing them that if they listen, it will do them good. It's a real challenge to prepare an effective introduction, but with the Lord's help and the exercise of a sanctified imagination, it can be done.

D. L. Moody once opened a sermon with, "I do not think there is a word in the English language so little understood as the word *Gospel.*" J. Wallace Hamilton began a message with, "Conspicuous among the many by-products of the machine age is the rise to royalty of the repairman. We ordinary people are almost wholly at his mercy." He then preached from Jeremiah 18:4 (KJV), "so he made it again." G. A. Studdert-Kennedy opened an Ascension Day message with, "He ascended into heaven. Did he? Where is heaven? What is it? Is it a place? Can we know what it is or where it is?"

These three examples introduce rule number one for the introduction: *Plan to hit the pulpit running.* Design that first sentence so it will grab the attention of the congregation and hold it. The day of the casual, unplanned, rambling introduction is over: "Now if you were with us three weeks ago when I started this series, you may recall . . ." Or, "Now if you'll take your Bibles and turn to the Epistle of Jude, right next to the Book of Revelation . . ." Preachers are heralds of the King and we don't have time to saunter through the introduction. If you want to say something about the weather or local events, do it at some other time. Years of experience in radio ministry have taught me the importance of those first few sentences in getting people to listen. They can turn us off very quickly, even if they're sitting in the pews looking at us.

There was a time when people expected sermons to have long introductions that included the background of the text, a few exegetical matters, and what other preachers have said about the passage. Those introductions assured the congregation that their pastor had done his homework, but those days are gone forever. Long and learned introductions that review past material are fine for Bible classes and lecture halls, but not for ministers in the pulpit who have thirty minutes to raise the dead. We live in the day of fast foods, digests, and sound bites, and the sooner we get down to business in the pulpit, the more successful that business will be. If you must refer to material presented in previous sermons, do it in the body of the sermon as though it were new material. If you use the word *remember*, those who don't remember or didn't hear it to begin with will be embarrassed, and those who do remember may feel proud. Either way, you've done more harm than good.

Turn on your right brain, ponder the text and the proposition, and imagine the best way to open the sermon. Let's consider the first outline on 1 John 1:5–10 and think about *deception*. Truth is the cement that holds society together, whether it's a marriage vow at the altar or a campaign promise at a political rally. Smooth-talking con artists are robbing elderly people of their savings, and scams of all kinds abound. There's a cry for integrity in government and in the church, yet many citizens believe that there's no relationship between an official's work and his or her character—or lack of it.

Write down phrases and quotations that come to your mind. "Remember the eleventh commandment: Thou shalt not get caught." Recall Oscar Wilde's novel *The Picture of Dorian Gray,* the story of an evil man who stayed young and handsome while his hidden portrait became uglier the more he sinned. An English proverb says: A clean glove often hides a dirty hand. Solomon wrote, "He who conceals his sins does not prosper" (Prov. 28:13). You have no doubt had some painful experience with a liar.

Here's one approach: "All of us want to live in a peaceful community and a safe neighborhood. What makes this possible? Good laws are important and so is good enforcement of those laws. But according to Scripture, the cement that holds things together—friendships, families, churches, communities, and even nations—is truth. If that's an accurate analysis, and I believe it is, then deception is the most dangerous virus we can ever encounter."

Let's refine it: "What's the cement that holds society together—our friendships, families, neighborhoods, churches, communities, and even nations? The answer may shock you. It's truth; that's right, truth. The most dangerous virus we can encounter in the world today is deception."

Sometimes an arresting quotation will get their attention: "Perhaps when you were in school, you had to learn two lines of poetry from Sir Walter Scott: 'O what a tangled web we weave / When first we practice to deceive.' Another writer added: 'But when we've practiced quite a while / How vastly we improve our style!' An accomplished hypocrite is a dangerous person to have around, and yet people are moving in that direction and don't realize it."

One of the greatest encouragements I ever received in my years of preaching came from a lad about ten years old who approached me after a worship service, looked up at me, and said, "I understood every word you said." It was like getting the Pulitzer prize. We preach to be understood, and that involves clear thinking, careful preparation, and organization—and the kind of delivery that makes people want to listen.

Six

We Preach
to Effect Change

Be transformed by the renewing of your mind.

Romans 12:2

"The concern is not to arrive at a definition and to close the book, but to arrive at an experience."[1] That statement was made about reading poetry but it applies to hearing sermons. Why? Because our goal in preaching is not just to provide religious education but to encourage spiritual transformation. When people listen to preaching, we want them to change by experiencing God through the Word and giving his spirit the freedom to make them more like Jesus Christ. We pray not only for a change in conduct but also for a change in character.

The prophet Jonah finally obeyed the Lord but not because he had experienced a change of heart. Even after the people of Nineveh repented, Jonah still despised them and wanted the Lord to destroy them. This reminds us that it isn't enough simply to *know* God's will or even to *do* God's will; we must "[do] the will of God *from the heart*" (Eph. 6:6 NASB, italics mine).

That's why Charles Simeon asked three questions of the sermons he preached: "Did it humble the sinner? Did it exalt the Savior? Did it promote holiness?"[2] Like every faithful preacher of the Word, he longed to see hearts and lives changed by the grace of God.

As encouraging as it may be week after week, it's too easy for us to be satisfied with ministering to appreciative listeners who compliment us on our preaching. "My test of the worth of a preacher," said Francis de Sales, "is when his congregations go away saying, not, 'What a beautiful sermon' but 'I will do something.'"[3] The Lord told the prophet Ezekiel, "My people come to you, as they usually do, and sit before you to listen to your words, but they do not put them into practice" (Ezek. 33:31). "Judas heard all of Christ's sermons," said Puritan preacher Thomas Goodwin, which is a solemn thought indeed.

What Kinds of Changes?

In preaching to effect change, we must be careful to deal with essentials and not incidentals or accidentals. A stewardship sermon ought to make people become more generous—and not just give more money, perhaps against their will. A challenge to discipleship should so present the Master in his wonder and beauty that people will want to follow him. Whether people need to change their schedules and pray more, lose their timidity and witness more, or give up their adult toys and serve more, the motivation must be Jesus Christ, not the persuasiveness of the preacher.

Paul gives us three pictures of the church in 1 Corinthians 3 that help us better understand the changes God wants to make in lives through the ministry of his Word.[4]

From Childhood to Maturity (1 Cor. 3:1-4)

The church is a family and the goal of every family is maturity. In spite of what doting grandparents may say, nobody wants a baby to stay a baby. We want the children to grow up and become responsible adults who can accept and wisely use the blessings and burdens of adulthood. It's the purpose of the family to love the children, protect them, train them, and help them mature; and in the realm of the spiritual, that's one of the purposes of the church.

A basic cause of trouble in the church at Corinth was the spiritual immaturity of some of the people. Like spoiled little children, there were those who wanted to be important, so they identified themselves with "great men" and developed a fan club mentality. Others got attention by flaunting their spiritual gifts, and still others by claiming their freedom and resisting the authority of God's apostle. Instead of developing an appetite for solid spiritual food, they lived on "baby food"; and instead of seeking to build up the church, they promoted themselves. There was no problem in the Corinthian church that maturity couldn't help to solve.

The faithful ministry of the Word encourages spiritual growth. It's the nourishment that God's children need and it leads to the discipline and exercise that should characterize mature believers. Paul summarized much of what this maturity looks like when he wrote 1 Corinthians 13, a chapter that ought to be read and pondered frequently by church members.

From Barrenness to Fruitfulness (1 Cor. 3:5-9a)

The local church is also a field, and the purpose of a field is a harvest. Each believer has his or her place to work in God's field: Some sow, others water, still others harvest the crop, but only God can make things grow. He assigns the task, he puts us where he wants us, and he gives us people to labor with in the field. You don't get a harvest without hard work, cooperation, and the blessing of God; and your goal is *quantity*.

What kind of "fruit" marks the maturing child of God? Certainly the fruit of the Spirit described in Galatians 5:22–23 reveal Christian character that glorifies God. It takes time to grow fruit and the preacher must not get impatient, "for at the proper time we will reap a harvest if we do not give up" (Gal. 6:9). And we need to keep in mind that we're not laboring alone, because others are also working in the field and encouraging the harvest (John 4:38).

Other spiritual fruit include winning the lost to Christ (John 4:35–38), encouraging one another in spiritual ministry (Rom. 1:11–13), holy living (Rom. 6:22), sharing material wealth (Rom. 15:25–28), doing the work God has assigned to us (Col. 1:10), and praising the Lord with "lips that confess his name" (Heb. 13:15). All of this is the "harvest of the Spirit" as people hear and receive the Word of God and obey what God says.

From the World's Wisdom to God's Wisdom (1 Cor. 3:9b-23)

The local church is a family and a field, but it's also a building; and as we and the congregation minister to the Lord, we're building a spiritual temple that will one day be tested by fire.[5] If we want our work to last, we must build on the right foundation, Jesus Christ (vv. 10–11); we must use the right materials (vv. 12–17); we must follow the right plan (vv. 18–20); and we must do everything with the right motive, which is the glory of God (vv. 21–23). The goal in building the local church is *quality*, a work that will endure the test of fire at the judgment seat of Christ.

To build on Jesus Christ means that everything that the church is and does is related directly to Christ, from preparing the budget to selecting the music for the congregation and choir. If you want it to last, you don't build a church on a preacher, a pet doctrine, or a denominational scheme. You build it on Jesus Christ. And if you want the work to last, you build with the right materials—the wisdom of God as found in the Word of God. This is represented by the "gold, silver, costly stones" that Paul mentioned (v. 12; see Prov. 2:1–6; 3:13–15; 8:10–11). The church at Corinth had been infected with man's wisdom, the philosophies of that day, and had ignored God's wisdom as taught in the Scriptures. Man's wisdom is like "wood, hay or straw" (1 Cor. 3:12): It's on the surface, it doesn't last, and it will one day be destroyed. God's wisdom is like gold, silver, and costly stones: You must dig for it in the Scriptures, it's beautiful and valuable, and it will stand the test of the fire. This is a solemn warning to those who preach clever sermons about trifling topics that attract crowds but don't build churches.

As people mature spiritually, they develop discernment and want for their church the things that please God, not the things that imitate the world or attract the worldly. The church doesn't have to imitate the world in order to influence the world. Paul makes it clear in this chapter that when the Spirit is at work, *there is no conflict in a local church between maturity, quantity, and quality because we're building to please Jesus Christ and glorify him.* Where there's maturity, there should be quality, and where there's quality, there should be quantity. Discipleship leads to service and service results in fruit.

The Tool for Change

Reviewing a bit of church history may help us better understand how the Spirit of God uses the Word to change lives. Paul had been falsely accused of encouraging the Gentile churches to abandon the law and even to break the law (Rom. 3:8; 6:1; Acts 21:27–28). When the legalists invaded the church at Corinth, Paul found it necessary to remind the believers of some basic theology about law and grace. The tools for spiritual change are the Word of God and prayer, as used by the Spirit in the hearts of God's worshiping, fellowshipping, and serving people. In 2 Corinthians 3,[6] Paul described his ministry of grace and contrasted it with the ministry of law and he used three vivid illustrations to explain what the Spirit does when we preach the Word of God's grace in the power of the Spirit.

Writing a Letter (vv. 1-6)

At Sinai, God wrote the law on tablets of stone, but since Pentecost he's been writing his Word on the hearts of his people.[7] *Spiritual transformation comes from within, from the heart.* If we preach the Word in the power of the Spirit, the Spirit writes that Word on the hearts of those who listen by faith, and it changes their character and conduct. Not many of us would go to the nearest hospital and volunteer to do a heart operation, but writing the Word on human hearts is even more serious because it carries eternal consequences. No wonder Paul asked, "And who is equal to such a task?" (2 Cor. 2:16). We must so preach in the power of the Spirit that the Word is received in hearts; otherwise, nothing will be changed.

Actually, there are three "heart letters" involved here: (1) the Corinthian saints were written on Paul's heart because of his love for them; (2) the Spirit was writing the Word on the hearts of the responsive believers; and (3) the church in its life and ministry was writing a letter that the unregenerate world would read. If the pastor loves the people and the people love the Word, then the church will "write a letter" that will influence the world for Christ.

Removing a Veil (vv. 7-16)

The ministry of law was associated with glory, but it wasn't a glory that lasted. The dramatic events at Sinai became memories, and even the glory on the face of Moses faded away. When Moses talked with the people, he had to wear a veil so they wouldn't see the glory disappearing; for, after all, who wants to follow a leader who is losing his glory? But the glory associated with God's grace is a glory that becomes greater and greater ("with ever-increasing glory" v. 18) until one day God's people step into eternity and not only behold Christ's glory but share in it (John 17:22–24). We don't have anything to hide and we don't need masks![8]

Looking into the Mirror (vv. 17-18)

The ministry of the law was a ministry of death (vv. 6–7), but the ministry of grace is a ministry of life. When an old covenant Jew looked at the Ten Commandments, they only reminded him of his failures; but when believers look into the Word of God, they see the Son of God and all he is to them and does for them.[9] As they believe the Word and obey it, that Word imparts life and enables them to become more like Jesus Christ (v. 18).

In other words, when the Scriptures are preached in divine power, people will have the Word lovingly written on their hearts, they will take off their masks and radiate God's glory, and they will gaze on Christ in his Word and be transformed to become like him. These are the miracles that can occur each time God's people assemble, worship the Lord, and believingly hear his gracious truth. It is more than gathering more information from the Bible. It is experiencing God and his transforming power.

Mutual Ministry

This kind of ministry demands a preacher who is spiritually prepared to preach the Word and a congregation that is spiritually prepared to hear the Word. No heart surgeon would rush into the operating arena unprepared, nor would he or she want the patient to be unprepared. Yet week after week, both preachers and worshipers often fail to prepare themselves for their awesome meeting with God, and the result is that both worship and proclamation become routine and the Spirit can do no mighty work among us.

The church ministers to the preacher just as the preacher ministers to the church. The congregation must be able to say, "Now we are all here in the presence of God to listen to everything the Lord has commanded you to tell us" (Acts 10:33). And the preacher must be able to affirm "The Spirit of the Lord is on me, because he has anointed me to preach" (Luke 4:18). These are among the basic elements necessary for spiritual transformation of God's people. When both church and pastor have been praying, living in the Word, and seeking to serve Christ in the marketplace, then the Spirit has something to work with when the saints gather for worship.

Applying God's Word

John Wesley wrote in his journal for Sunday, June 13, 1779, "This very day I heard many excellent truths delivered in the kirk. But as there was no application, it was likely to do as much good as the singing of a lark." Classical homiletics calls for the minister to preach a sermon that includes exposition, illustration, and application, with the application usually at the end. "If there is no summons, there is no sermon," taught John Broadus, and the rallying cry became, "Preach for a verdict!" To the orthodox, biblical preaching consisted of proclaiming *(kerygma)*, explaining *(didache)*, discussing *(homilia)*, and exhorting or applying *(paradesis)*.

A Different Approach

Things began to change, however, and the popular approach became: The Bible makes its own application. All the preacher had to do was read the text, explain it, moralize a bit, tell a few stories, and leave the rest to the Lord and the listener. And yet this approach seems contrary to the instructions given us in the Pastoral Epistles and the examples found throughout the Bible. Paul emphasized not only the proclamation of the Word but also the teaching of doctrine and the application of doctrine to the life of the church and the individual believer. The prophets weren't content to thunder the message; they also released a few lightning bolts of application and warning. And doesn't our Lord's Sermon on the Mount conclude with an admonition to obey what Jesus taught?

If you doubt the authority of God's Word, then you won't apply it and perhaps shouldn't even be preaching it. If you worry about pleasing people in a pluralistic society and maintaining a politically correct stance, then by all means stay away from personal applications of the Scripture. If your sermons are religious essays on current affairs, then there won't be much to apply. But if you preach the Word, depend on the Holy Spirit, love Jesus Christ and your people, and realize that your time of ministry is short, you will want to make the truth of God personal and practical to the listeners. Yes, the Word does impress itself on the heart, and the Holy Spirit does convict, but the Word needs a preacher, and the Spirit needs a voice, and therefore the sermon needs an application.

What Is "Application"?

Our English word *apply* comes from the Latin and means "to fold, to bring together." When we apply the Scriptures, we bring truth and life together so the message is practical and we also bring the people and God's Word together so the message is personal. We follow the pattern set by Paul of bringing doctrine and duty together and daring to say, "therefore." Applications are really God's invitations for people to change, grow, and experience new blessings from God.

Must the application always be made at the close of the sermon? Not necessarily, unless we're addressing a hostile audience and gradually working toward that final challenge, or if the message will be more effective if we save the major thrust for the final minutes. In the course of the weekly exposition of Scripture, the minister will lovingly apply the Word as the sermon progresses—promises, warnings, precepts, principles—and then pull it together at the close, trusting to stir the listeners' hearts and capture their wills for Christ. Even if we preach to the same congregation week after week, each sermon is different and each preaching situation is unique, and the wise preacher will skillfully use the sword of the Spirit to pierce and the medicine of the Word to heal (Ps. 107:20).

In applying the Word, we must be precise and practical so the people will know what to do and how to do it. It's better to make the appeal positive because people respond more readily to rewards than they do to punishments, although the negative warnings of Scripture must not be ignored. However, keep in mind that Isaiah's six "woes" in chapter 5 were preceded chronologically by his own "Woe is me!" expressed in chapter 6. We apply the sermon to ourselves before we apply it to others.

Illustrations—Pro and Con

Traditionally ministers have put illustrations into their preaching for the same reason cooks put spices into their cooking—to make it more palatable. The preacher would look at the outline and decide where it needed spicing up and then find just the right story or quotation to do the job. But this traditional homiletical approach of "explanation, illustration, application" has almost disappeared, and we should be thankful, because it was mechanical and predictable. It may have helped to sell illustration books, but the illustrations didn't always help the message.

When it comes to illustrating the sermon, I'm somewhat of a maverick. I believe that a sermon ought to be so luminous that we shouldn't have to add "windows" to let in the light. If we use illustrations at all, it's not to shed light on the obvious but to reach the imagination of our hearers and prepare the way for the reception of the truth.[10] Preaching ought to inform the mind, and if an illustration helps people understand Bible truth more easily, then use the illustration. How you use illustrations depends on your own skill and the kind of congregation you are addressing.

Preaching ought also to stir the imagination and the emotions, and it's here that illustrations can be valuable. "The human mind is not, as philosophers would have you think, a debating hall, but a picture gallery."[11] A striking quotation, a remarkable event, or a moving experience can so affect the imagination that the listener will be more disposed to accept God's Word. The proper use of imagery—similes, metaphors, symbols— is a skill the preacher should develop, because the Bible is filled with exciting imagery that helps us better understand God's truth. I'll talk more about this in chapter 11.

Our Lord's use of parables and imagery shouldn't be classified as giving illustrations because that's not what he was doing. Contrary to what Sunday school quarterlies say, parables are not "earthly stories with heavenly meanings." A parable begins as *a picture* of something we see in life, and it gets our attention; but then it becomes *a mirror* in which we see ourselves. We are in the parable! But finally, if we yield to the Spirit, the parable becomes a *window* through which we see God and learn about his love and grace. Ordinary stories don't do that!

Jesus was a master of the metaphor and the parable and he took this approach to open the eyes and ears of people to the truth (see Matthew 13:10–17). They were blind to the spiritual lessons in creation around them, so he spoke about seeds, soil, dogs and pigs, vines, yeast, birth, wineskins, and scores of other familiar things, always relating them to spiritual truth. He aroused the interest of the concerned and sought to help them hear and see spiritual truth. But at the same time, he passed judgment on those in the crowd who thought they already knew it all. By using parabolic imagery, Jesus opened the eyes of the blind and closed the eyes of those who thought they could see.

Where should we find illustrations? In the Bible, in personal experience, in biography and autobiography, and (if you are careful) in current events. I caution you to be careful in using current events because you can't always trust the news reports. As the story unfolds, it may take on a completely different meaning. Of course, the same warning applies when you use biographies and autobiographies, because even the best writers make mistakes. It's remarkable how one book perpetuates the errors of another book.

Cultivate the kind of homiletical intuition that jabs you and says, *This is a terrific illustration!* But if you use illustrations from real life, particularly from family experiences, be sure you get permission from the people involved. Your wife and children or favorite deacon may not want the story told to the whole world, so tread softly. More than one preacher's kid has resented being dragged into the sermon but never said anything about it.

The two worst sources of illustrations are illustration books and other preachers' sermons, especially if you try to deceive your people into thinking that the preacher's experience actually happened to you. There are readers in our congregations and they may just happen to have the same book in their library; but even if they don't, there's no place in the pulpit for plagiarism. As for illustration books, the stories are usually old and threadbare, copied from other books, or they're about people who aren't easily recognized today. The stories may have worked for D. L. Moody or Billy Sunday but they may not work for you.

Here are some suggestions regarding the use of illustrations that may save you some embarrassment.

- Use illustrations that are natural to you. I once used a story about a football game, and after the service, people asked me where I got it. They knew I didn't follow the sports scene and that the story had been borrowed.
- Select illustrations carefully and use them sparingly. Nobody wants to hear "skyscraper sermons"—one story on top of another. And be sure none of the illustrations could possibly be offensive because of race, economic status, vocation, or nationality.
- Document the illustration for future use. To write "Bob's story about the boat" on your outline is to court disaster if you want to preach the sermon a few years later, unless the story is unforgettable or you have a photographic memory.
- Use humor wisely and not at all in the conclusion of the message when you want people to be serious about obeying God's Word. There is a place for humor in the pulpit if you have a natural sense of humor, but don't become a religious stand-up comic.
- Don't repeat illustrations unless you're preaching to a parade or your people have bad memories. The stale apology "I may have told this before, but it bears repeating" doesn't absolve us. It only reveals that we were either too lazy or too unconcerned to find something new.

And Now in Conclusion . . .

Once more, I find myself differing from the classical homileticians who taught us to use the conclusion of the sermon to repeat the proposition and review the main points. Then we were to turn the proposition into an exhortation and, if there was time, add a story.

If our preaching has been clear, the people ought to know both the proposition and the main points of the message. Why insult their intelligence and short-term memory by giving a summary? And if we lovingly applied God's truth as we delivered the message, the congregation knows what God wants them to do. In fact the Spirit will say different things to different people, some of which may not have been in the sermon. Special messages may need summaries and exhortations, but pastoral preaching to a church family is different. At the close of our family meals, my wife didn't remind the children what they had eaten and why she had set it before them. They ate it, they enjoyed it, and it kept them healthy, even if two days later they couldn't tell you what the menu had been.

The best conclusion is the one that is brief, arresting, and makes obeying the truth so attractive and Jesus so worthy of obedience that nothing more needs to be said. To preach the sermon again, or to preach material we forgot to include earlier, is to tell everybody that we really didn't prepare. As with a business transaction or a lawyer's brief before a jury, the last few minutes can make the difference between success and failure, life and death. Prepare what you say carefully because you are preaching to bring about change to the glory of God.

Seven

We Preach from the Overflow

> When I let my heart grow cold, my preaching is cold; and when it is confused, my preaching is confused.
>
> Richard Baxter
> *The Reformed Pastor*

"As dull as a sermon" is to me an uncomfortable simile that ought to be expunged from every thesaurus. (I've been guilty of preaching dull sermons and I've paid for it by having to *listen* to dull sermons.) It's only during these latter years of my ministry, however, that I've discovered why some sermons are dull and others are interesting. It has nothing to do with the *science* of preaching and everything to do with the *art* of preaching. If we want to be interesting and therefore communicate the Word with greater skill, *we must preach from the overflow.*

The Preacher as Artist

What we call "homiletics" is simply the science of preaching. It can be learned by reading books, attending classes, and listening to the best preachers. However, filling your notebook or computer with words, successfully passing examinations, and finally graduating from the course is no guarantee that your sermons will automatically be interesting. If medical students stopped their training immediately after passing the anatomy courses, they'd be ill equipped to deal with the needs of living people. T. S. Eliot reminds us that "a study of anatomy will not teach you how to make a hen lay eggs."[1] Being a successful chicken farmer involves knowing something about life.

Every science has an art, and it's the art of doing something that brings out the individuality of the worker and makes his or her work unique and therefore interesting. Because no two painters paint alike, you can tell a Picasso from a Van Gogh. Knowing the distinctive style of various musicians enables you to identify who is singing or playing. A gifted performer could easily imitate another performer, but that's not how real art works. As soon as artists discover their true "voice"—who they are and how they're supposed to express it—they're able to combine their talent, training, and artistic intuition and begin performing creatively.

In short, we don't preach out of the abundance of our library but "out of the overflow of the heart" (Matt. 12:34). Real preaching comes from the overflow. "Above all else," counseled Solomon, "guard your heart, for it is the wellspring of life" (Prov. 4:23). Creativity depends a great deal on receptivity, which means being open to God, to life, and to people. Unless there's a spiritual overflow in our lives, ministry will be dry and fruitless.

The Shame of Shallowness

Certainly God calls his people to experience a life of depth, and we shepherds can't easily lead the flock where we've never been ourselves. The Lord wants his truth to penetrate the inner being (Ps. 51:6); he wants us to lay deep foundations for our lives (Luke 6:48). The Spirit longs to give us the kind of depth Paul prayed for in Ephesians 3:14–21, a prayer we would do well to pray frequently for ourselves as well as for our people.

God's invitation to depth is too often drowned out by the world's temptation to the superficial. We live in a shallow society that delights in flitting around on the surface of things and living on substitutes. Believers are supposed to be like trees (Ps. 1:3), not like rootless tumbleweeds being blown about by every puff of wind. Population mobility makes it easy for the preacher to recycle his material, and if he runs out, there are plenty of sermon cassettes and sermon outline books to replenish the supply. You can even subscribe to services that will provide you with weekly sermon outlines at a price and you can find free material just waiting online on your computer. The opportunities are limitless for the shallow preacher to manufacture a ministry that's a mile long and an inch thick.

What are some of the marks of a shallow preaching ministry? One of them is preparing predictable sermons that are easy to listen to because nobody is afraid that the Spirit will bring conviction. After all, if the preacher wasn't disturbed when he prepared the sermon, why should the congregation be disturbed when they hear it? The sermon is harmless because the congregation knows what's coming next. Biblical sermons are supposed to be like a doctor's prescription, designed especially for the patients; but shallow ministry provides generic messages that fit everybody comfortably. The emphasis is on externals; there's no challenge for change and nobody goes away upset. A good time was had by all and it's safe to return next week.

Another characteristic of ministry that lacks depth is that it offers superficial solutions to serious problems. Like the false prophets in Jeremiah's time, shallow preachers "dress the wounds of . . . people as though it were not serious. 'Peace, peace,' they say, when there is no peace" (Jer. 6:14). It's frightening to hear Jesus say that "many" will claim to be true believers on the day of judgment but that he will have to reject them because they never really trusted him (Matt. 7:21–23). We want to prepare messages that penetrate the heart, not tickle the ears.

A third characteristic of shallow ministry is the absence of new church problems that come from people responding to new challenges. It's business as usual in the church, week after week. But the Lord wants his people to be courageous pioneers and not comfortable settlers. God's word to the preacher is, "Be diligent in these matters; give yourself wholly to them, so that everyone may see your progress" (1 Tim. 4:15). The Greek word translated "progress" *(prokope)* means "pioneer advance." It's the picture of fearless people "cutting forward" through every obstacle and blazing new trails so that others may follow. "It is inspiring to see a young preacher grow," wrote A. T. Robertson, "for then the church will grow with him."[2] It's even more inspiring to see an experienced older preacher *keep on growing*, for then the church won't settle for what Dr. Robert A. Cook used to call "sanctified senility." The same pioneer advance that characterizes the preacher should also characterize the congregation (Phil. 1:25). A local church should be a launching pad, not a parking lot.

Dig Deep

The wise preacher is like the man who when he built his house "dug down deep" (Luke 6:48). Depth in preaching doesn't mean obscurity, as though our aim is to confuse people or impress them. Depth in preaching means that we *make the profound things simple, the simple things profound, and all things practical.* Surface preachers are satisfied with outlines, stories, academic explanations, and surface applications; but depth preachers want to stir the heart, excite the imagination, and eventually capture the will. As Halford Luccock wrote, "The purpose of preaching is not to make people see reasons, but visions."[3] Their request is, "We would like to see Jesus" (John 12:21).

What is required of us if we're to have this kind of ministry? I believe a ministry of depth begins with *our own deepening relationship with God,* as we saw Paul praying for in Ephesians 3:14–21. It's frightening how many ministers don't cultivate a consistent, disciplined devotional life; and some of them excuse this failure by arguing that their sermon preparation amounts to the same thing. But it doesn't. Cooks who prepare meals for others but who rarely take time to feed themselves will eventually suffer from malnutrition. Preparing sermons can nourish us to some degree, but it's not the same as spending uninterrupted time with God, hearing him speak through the Word, worshiping him, and sharing our needs with him. It's important that we take time to prepare messages, but it's also important that we "take time to be holy."

I admit that the preacher has some unique obstacles to overcome in developing a satisfying devotional life, not the least of which is the danger of *professionalism.* As ministers, we're familiar with the Bible, not only because of our training but also because we use the Scriptures daily as we study, counsel, and minister. If we aren't careful, our use of God's Word can become professional and we'll turn *the* Book into *a* book and gradually lose the delight and dynamic that come when we read the Bible with expectant hearts. George Macdonald said, "Nothing is so deadening to the divine as an habitual dealing with the outsides of holy things."[4] So, we must take care to get *inside* the Word and let the Word get into us (Col. 3:16).

We must come to our daily devotional time, not as professional Christian workers who need something to say at the next meeting, but as sinners who desperately need God's grace. We must never lose the wonder of the Word of God or of the remarkable fact that the Father wants to speak to creatures like us. We need to cultivate an appetite for God's truth and believe our Lord's promise, "Blessed are those who hunger and thirst for righteousness, for they will be filled" (Matt. 5:6). As with the body, so with the soul: When you start to lose your appetite, it's a sign you're getting sick. Deal with the sickness and your appetite will return.

A second obstacle to our devotional life is *intimidation.* We feel guilty because we don't have the profound spiritual experiences of the great men and women of God we've heard about and read about. We try to imitate their holy disciplines only to falter, and then we wonder if we even have the right to preach about the spiritual life when we feel like such miserable failures.

Well, be of good cheer! Each of us is unique and our Father doesn't require us to imitate one another. Abraham talked with God the way two neighbors might chat over the back fence (Gen. 18:16–33), but Moses interceded on Mount Sinai in the presence of God's awesome glory. Joshua saw God demolish the walls of Jericho, but the great apostle Paul was smuggled over the wall of Damascus in a basket (Acts 9:25). The apostles performed miracles, but the greatest of the prophets, John the Baptist, never performed a miracle; yet his witness to Christ bore fruit even after he was dead (Matt. 11:11; John 10:41). In your daily worship time, be yourself, be open and honest with God, don't be in a hurry, and let him do for you what he knows is best. If we preach a text that's beyond our experience, let's be honest enough to admit it and preach with humility. Otherwise we may find ourselves lagging behind our conscience and becoming like Ananias and Sapphira who tried to make people think they were more spiritual than they really were.

One of the most aggravating obstacles to successful meditation and prayer is *the intrusion of good thoughts.* As we're pondering the Word, we get an idea for a sermon, or we think of somebody for whom we promised to pray, or we suddenly remember a job to be done that day. We're never sure whether such thoughts are the Holy Spirit's reminders or the devil's attacks. If we entertain these visitors too long, we'll probably go off on detours and dissipate whatever the Spirit has done for us so far. The solution is simple: Write down the sermon idea on a piece of paper and drop it in the "idea" folder, pause to pray for the person in need, write the job to be done in your date book, and then get back to meditation and prayer. When it comes to the devotional life, ministers must be like athletes in training and say, "This one thing I do!"

The message the Emmaus disciples brought to the frightened believers in Jerusalem is a good model for us to follow today: Their witness was born out of their own experience with Jesus, it burned in their hearts, it was the result of understanding the Scriptures, and it proclaimed the living Christ (Luke 24:13–35). When God's Spirit lights a flame in our hearts by opening our eyes and opening the Scriptures, we'll have no problem opening our lips and preaching Christ. "I like the idea of pouring our sermons out of our own hearts," said Charles Spurgeon. "They must come from our hearts, or they will not go to our hearers' hearts."[5]

Overflow of Heart and Mind

Not only must God's Word enrich our hearts (Col. 3:16), but our studies must also enrich our minds. Preachers must be readers and should read widely and not just for message preparation. Since all truth is God's truth and all truth intersects, any subject we study can throw light on the Bible, the people we're working with, the ministry we do, or life itself. "Reading maketh a full man,"[6] wrote Frances Bacon, and you need to be full to experience overflow.

However, there's a difference between diligent preachers who grow because they read and "bookish" preachers who read but don't grow. All they do is "swell" and bore people with what they think they know. Bookish preachers impress you with what they claim they've read but they don't come across as people who have assimilated what they've read and made it a part of life and ministry. They tell you they keep up with all the best-sellers, as though that were important, but they aren't always acquainted with the classics, the books of the ages that will outlast the books of the hour. The poet Alexander Pope described this kind of person in his "Essay on Criticism" as

> The bookful blockhead, ignorantly read,
> With loads of learned lumber in his head.

We must read widely but we must not take our reading undigested into the pulpit. Writing about his own preaching, John Wesley said, "I design plain truth for plain people. . . . Nay, my design is, in some sense, to forget all that ever I have read in my life."[7]

Your mind grows by taking in and your heart by giving out, so keep in balance. As you read various kinds of books, copy material that you see is useful, document it, and share it with your people. Filter everything through the grid of the Word of God and keep in mind that you can learn from people you disagree with. Be a seeker of truth with God's truth leading the way and in his light you will see light (Ps. 36:9).

If you store your heart with the Word of God and your mind with the best thoughts of the best writers and thinkers, you'll have a well of wisdom that will overflow when you need it. If you keep an organized file or journal of the best ideas you meet as you read, carefully documenting them so you can give credit, it will serve you well. A large library isn't always evidence of an enlarged mind. Make the best use of the books you have and let them become part of you. More books and articles are published in one day than you and I could read in a lifetime, so don't feel you have to read everything. Books that excite other people may bore you, but don't apologize. Books are like tools, and every workman has to fit the tool to his training and experience as well as to the job being tackled. In time, you will grow to appreciate the better books, so be patient with yourself.

Undertows and Deserts

My wife and I were listening to a preacher who is a friend and a capable exegete, but something was wrong. The longer he introduced the message, the more uncomfortable I felt; and finally I said to my wife, "He's not preaching from the overflow. He's preaching from the undertow. He's angry." And as he preached, the more evident his anger became.

Undertows are strong currents beneath the water, moving in an opposite direction from the current on the surface. They occur not only in oceans but also in the deepest levels of our human psyche. An aquatic undertow can perform a service by carrying away the flotsam and jetsam the waves deposit on the shore, but human undertows don't work that way. Instead of removing debris, human undertows contribute to our internal rubbish and make it difficult for the overflow to function.

The undertow may be from any number of causes—pride, anger, envy, unconfessed sin, disturbed human relationships, even bad attitudes about the sermon or the service—but whatever the cause, it has to be dealt with. Sometimes we recognize the problem and sincerely turn to the Lord for help, but sometimes we don't detect either the symptoms or the causes, and that's when undertows are dangerous. There's a fine line between the carnal and the spiritual, and we may think we're motivated by the zeal of the Lord when it's really a ruptured and bloated ego at work.

The greatest damage from personal undertows isn't the short-term interruption of the flow of the Holy

Spirit, as serious as that is. It's the long-term blockage of spiritual power that turns the river into a desert. "Dry seasons" in ministry may have more than one cause—emotional and physical weariness, sickness, even discouragement—but one of the common causes is the increase of inner rubbish that builds a dam to prevent the flow of the Holy Spirit. That rubbish might include things like an undisciplined devotional life, broken relationships in the home or within the circle of church leaders, promises not kept, and work not done. To make matters worse, we start lying about these things, first lying to others and then lying to ourselves, and the vital juices begin to dry up quickly (Ps. 32:1–5).

Creativity in spiritual things depends on a right relationship with God, ourselves, other people, and our work. Any ruptures will gradually replace creativity with mere religious activity, then counterfeit religious activity, and finally disintegration will lead to collapse. We need to deal with the problem before it gets that far. Blessed is that servant who has a loved one or friend to turn to for confidential help and encouragement.

Graciously the Holy Spirit ministers to and through those servants who sincerely seek God's best for themselves and their people and who are willing to pay the price to receive it. The Lord's promise is, "I will pour water on the thirsty land, and streams on the dry ground; I will pour out my Spirit on your offspring, and my blessing on your descendents" (Isa 44:3).

Eight

We Preach as
an Act of Worship

> No man can bear witness to Christ and to himself at the same time. No man can give the impression that he himself is clever and that Christ is mighty to save.
>
> James Denny

The most complete definition of worship I've found is by William Temple, who served as Archbishop of Canterbury from 1942 to 1944. Temple writes:

> For to worship is to quicken the conscience by the holiness of God, to feed the mind with the truth of God, to purge the imagination by the beauty of God, to open the heart to the love of God, to devote the will to the purpose of God.[1]

If you change the word *worship* to *preach,* the definition will still apply, because faithful preaching and spiritual worship involve the same elements. Therefore, we must not put asunder what God has joined together—preaching and worship. The sequence of activities that occurs before the minister steps into the pulpit must not be called "preliminaries" and looked on only as religious exercises to dispense with as quickly as possible. If the preacher and the sermon are what they ought to be, the worship that has already started simply continues when the preacher delivers the message; for in worship we ought to preach (1 Peter 2:9) and in preaching we ought to worship.

Sometimes you hear people say, "I don't go to church to hear a sermon. I go to church to worship God." The statement sounds very pious but it's dead wrong. (I'm never sure if they say this to excuse their pastor's poor preaching or their own poor listening.) As a holy priesthood, the church at worship offers up "spiritual sacrifices" to the Lord (1 Peter 2:5), including our bodies (Rom 12:1), our prayers (Ps. 141:1–2), our praises (Heb. 13:15), and our material gifts (Phil. 4:18).

But paying attention to the reading and preaching of the Word of God is also an offering to the Lord. Twice in Romans Paul used the word *latreuo* to describe his preaching ministry (1:9; 15:16), a word that's associated with ministry at the altar. In fact the NIV translates Romans 15:16 "with the priestly duty of proclaiming the gospel of God." In other words, when we preach the Word in the Spirit's power, we aren't just standing in a pulpit, addressing people; we're standing at an invisible altar, worshiping God.

"The sermon is an integral part of worship," wrote J. I. Packer. "Great heights of adoration, praise and worship can be reached by a devout congregation during the sermon as the things of God pass before them."[2] But for preaching to be an act of worship, the preacher must meet certain conditions.

Living as a Worshiper

Worship isn't a role that we play once a week; it's a life that we live all the time. Worship doesn't stop when we finish our morning devotional time or when we retire for the night. We ought to go to sleep praising God and meditating on his Word, planning to awaken the next day still praying and praising. As we perform our daily tasks, we need to keep our hearts open to God and be sensitive to the leading of the Spirit. If every Sunday morning we have to go through extensive alterations before we can step into the pulpit, then we ought to either stay out of the pulpit or never leave it.

The services we render in pastoral ministry ought to be given to God as acts of worship, including the responsibilities we don't especially enjoy. That means doing our work for Jesus' sake and not to please our people or ourselves. God wants to be glorified in the Thursday evening committee meeting as much as in the Sunday morning choir anthem. It takes time, but we need to teach our people that "administration" is just a more sophisticated way of saying "ministry." Since God is present when only two or three of his people meet in his name, then we can worship him in a hospital room, at a restaurant table, or while sitting in a meeting.

To live daily as a worshiper doesn't mean becoming one of those saints whom D. L. Moody described as "so heavenly minded they're no earthly good." It's just the opposite: Nobody is more aware of people and their needs, more alert to opportunities, and more motivated to serve than the believer who abides "in the shadow of the Almighty" (Ps. 91:1).

Studying and Preparing as a Worshiper

Several attitudes are involved in the way we study and prepare, not the least of which is *our attitude toward worship*. If the word "preliminaries" crosses our mind, we need to go to the altar and confess our sin. If our choice of the songs and readings is governed only by the theme of the sermon, we need a much wider view of congregational praise. If we get upset when somebody uses the word *liturgy*, we need to be reminded that every church has a liturgy, either a good one or a bad one. After all, the word simply means "an order of service" and comes from the Greek word *leitourgia*, which means "to discharge a public duty." It's used for priestly ministry in Luke 1:23; 2 Corinthians 9:12; and Hebrews 8:6; 9:21. Paul used it to refer to the offering he was receiving for the Jerusalem poor. Some churches have a more elaborate liturgy than others, but all churches need a liturgy or the congregation won't be able to worship together.

A second consideration is *our attitude toward the Scriptures*. Is the Bible only a book from which we select religious ideas to talk about or is it the authoritative Word of God by which God's people must live, serve, worship, and die? How can we worship God if we don't know who he is and what he requires of us? If preaching is to be a part of worship, then we must approach the Scriptures with a worshipful spirit, full of wonder at the greatness of the Word of God and the awesomeness of the God of the Word. This means accepting the paradoxes and mysteries in Scripture and not trying to explain everything. When Paul finished his profound discussion of Israel, God's electing grace, and the church (Rom. 9–11), he went from theology to doxology: "Oh, the depth of the riches of the wisdom and knowledge of God!" (Rom. 11:33). He didn't solve every problem or answer every question but he did point us to God and lead us to worship him.

Our attitude toward study affects how we prepare. Some preachers can hardly wait to get into the study, open their books, and begin to dig into the rich mine of Scripture, and very unwillingly do they leave the study to go about their pastoral work. Other ministers go to the study reluctantly, praying that there will be enough interruptions to make the morning tolerable. If, however, studying the Word means worshiping the Lord, then the study becomes a holy of holies where his glory shines on the sacred page. "They feast on the abundance of your house; you give them drink from your river of delights. For with you is the fountain of life; in your light we see light" (Ps. 36:8–9).

We also need to think about *our attitude toward the sermon itself.* If preaching is indeed an act of worship, then the sermon itself is our sacrifice to the Lord; *and we want to give him our very best.* Like David we affirm, "I will not take for the LORD what is yours, or sacrifice a burnt offering that costs me nothing" (1 Chron. 21:24). The first clause steers us away from plagiarism and the second clause discourages laziness. Under the Old Testament economy, each sacrifice brought to the altar was carefully examined lest the worshipers keep the best for themselves and give the rejects to the Lord (Mal. 1:6–9). This can happen in the study. Granted, there are weeks when the demands are many and the days are long, and we know we've not had time to give our very best to sermon preparation; but the Lord knows all about it and will help us just the same. It's when we *have* the time and don't use it wisely that we bring an inadequate sacrifice to the altar. Let's be diligent in our studies, for even when we've done our best, we still feel like unprofitable servants.

Finally, but not least important, we must consider *our attitude toward the congregation.* Said Arthur Teikmanis, "Dynamic preaching is basically pastoral care in the context of worship."[3] We want to preach messages that will enable the people to see God more clearly and worship him more sincerely. Seeing the Lord "high and exalted" is their first step toward solving every problem and taking new steps of faith, and we don't want to rob the flock of those gifts from the Lord. It's an awesome thing to stand before God's people and declare God's message.

The message we prepare and the way we deliver it will let them know whether or not we love them, know their needs, and really care about them.

Leading the Congregation as a Worshiper

Ministers who elevate themselves above their congregation when they preach need to cultivate the attitude John Wesley expressed in his journal entry for November 8, 1738: "In the evening I proclaimed mercy to my fellow-sinners at Basingshaw church. . . ."[4] Identification with the congregation is important, for even though ministers are the appointed shepherds, they're also sheep in the flock. We must preach to our own hearts in the study if we hope to reach our listeners' hearts in the sanctuary. In recent years, preachers have started sitting with the people in the congregation before going to the platform to preach, a practice I sincerely approve. If pastors also serve as worship leaders, they can't do this; but they can strive to lead the congregation as fellow-worshipers and fellow-sinners.

The atmosphere of worship should combine sobriety with joy, what the psalmist had in mind when he wrote, "Serve the LORD with fear and rejoice with trembling" (Ps. 2:11; and see 97:1; 99:1). Sober Christians are serious about the things of the Lord but not so solemn that they can't express joy. Those who lead us in worship—and this includes the preacher—must be very careful not to turn the sanctuary into a theater and worship into entertainment. In Scripture the people who met God didn't go away laughing.

Preaching as a Worshiper

James Denney said it best:

> If the sermon in church is what it ought to be—if it is not an exhibition of the preacher but of Jesus—there should be nothing in it even conceivably in contrast with worship, but the very reverse. What can be more truly described as worship than hearing the Word of God as it ought to be heard, hearing it with penitence, with contrition, with faith and self-consecration, with vows of new obedience? If this is not worship in spirit and in truth, what is?[5]

One day we'll be judged for our hearing as well as our speaking, so all of us need to heed our Lord's admonition, "Therefore consider carefully how you listen" (Luke 8:18). Congregations in the first century had to listen carefully when the Word was publicly read and preached because the people didn't own copies of the Scriptures and there was no equipment to record the messages. We have both Bibles and recording equipment in our churches today and we can, therefore, actually postpone listening to the sermon. But listening to a sermon cassette while we're driving down the highway or jogging through the park isn't quite the same as listening while in the context of worship. I'm not opposed to people listening to taped messages; I'm concerned about people possibly missing the immediate impact of the spoken Word that comes as we listen worshipfully with the rest of God's people.

Our people need to learn how to listen as worshipers and not as students or critics who are so busy writing down the outline that they completely miss the message. Anything in our preaching that calls attention to itself, and that includes our clever outlines and asides, will take the attention of the people away from the Word of God; and that defeats the purpose of preaching. As we preach God's truth, we must do so as in the presence of the Lord of Hosts, for God is listening. The words we speak and the way we speak them become an offering to the Lord, and we want to give him our best.

Hugh Latimer was to preach before the King of England. As he made his way to the palace, he said that he seemed to hear a voice saying, "Latimer! Latimer! Be careful what you preach today! You are preaching to the King of England." But then he seemed to hear another voice that said, "Latimer! Latimer! Be careful what you preach today! You are preaching before the King of Kings!"[6]

If we keep that in mind as we prepare and proclaim, our preaching will truly be an act of worship to the glory of God and the edifying of his people.

We Preach Depending on God's Power

After all our preparation, general and special for the conduct of public worship and for preaching, our dependence for real success is on the Spirit of God.

John A. Broadus
A Treatise on the Preparation and Delivery of Sermons

"The pastor would like to thank Brother McGuire for rewiring the pulpit." I read that statement in a bulletin somebody left in a hymnal in a church we were visiting, and immediately I gave thanks for Brother McGuire. On more than one occasion the pulpit I was in had needed rewiring because this preacher was out of power.

No matter how talented, gifted, or well trained our people may think we are, we who preach the Word know that we can't do it alone. I'll quote Paul's question again: "And who is equal to such a task?" (2 Cor. 2:16). We've confessed more than once, "I'm not!"

When Jesus said, "Apart from me you can do nothing" (John 15:5), he was speaking to us; and we've learned from sad experience the truth of his words.

Hear a parable! A minister was heading for a preaching engagement, but Satan got there first. Masquerading as the announced preacher, Satan stood in the pulpit, read the text, and proceeded to preach an orthodox Christian sermon. The preacher met Satan after the service and asked, "Weren't you afraid to preach orthodox doctrine?" Satan smiled and replied, "Not at all, because my preaching can't affect anybody. You see, *I don't have any unction.*"

The Power of the Holy Spirit

Few things in ministry are as uncomfortable and discouraging as trying to travel "on empty" in public, and that's what happens when we lack unction in the pulpit. I once heard A. W. Tozer say, "If God were to take the Holy Spirit out of this world, most of what the church is doing would go right on and nobody would know the difference." My head nodded in agreement as my heart wept in remembrance. Whatever else our churches may be known for today, we're not especially recognized as repositories of spiritual power. The early church moved forward victoriously because the believers were energized by the Holy Spirit and motivated by a love for Christ, and there's no reason why our churches can't follow their example today.

God doesn't enlist his servants to abandon us; he wants to enable and equip us for the tasks he's called us to do. Before he sent Gideon to fight the Midianites, the Lord clothed the frightened farmer with the Holy Spirit (Judg. 6:34). Jesus depended on the Holy Spirit from his conception and birth (Luke 1:35) to his death on the cross (Heb. 9:14) and throughout his entire ministry (Acts 10:38). He admonished his disciples not to begin their own ministries until first they had been "clothed with power from on high" (Luke 24:49).

The church of Acts 1 is "The Church of the Closed Door." The description is that of the average church today: enjoying fellowship, praying, searching the Scriptures, and electing officers. But when the Holy Spirit filled the believers on the Day of Pentecost, the doors were opened and God's church began to impact the city and the world. To see the difference the Holy Spirit makes when he empowers God's people, compare Acts 1:12–26 with Acts 2:42–47.

Equipping

How does the Holy Spirit help us in our preaching? To begin with, he gave us our call and equipped us with the gifts he wants us to have and use. Years ago Dr. Torrey Johnson said to me, "Find the one thing you do that God blesses and stay with it." Is your preaching gift that of an evangelist? Then use it as widely as you can, but don't neglect teaching the new converts and encouraging them in the battles of life. Are you gifted as a teacher? Then feed the lambs and the sheep, but always share the gospel and tell people how to be saved. Is your pulpit ministry primarily exhortation? Then exhort in the power of the Spirit, always basing duty on doctrine and always making Christ the motive for service and holy living.

Enlightening

The Holy Spirit also assists us in understanding the Word as we study. God has given teachers to the church— and we need to hear them and read what they've written—but ultimately only the Spirit can make God's truth meaningful in our lives and ministries. We want to be "Spirit taught" and not "man taught." It's good to read what scholars have written in books—and I do it constantly—but it's also good to let the Spirit enlighten our hearts (Eph. 1:15–23) and write the truth there as well (2 Cor. 3:1–3). No matter what others have written for our learning, there's a freshness about the ministry of a Spirit-taught minister who is marked by the oil of God on his head. Robert Murray M'Cheyne used to write "Help, Lord!" in the margins of his sermon manuscript to remind him to cry out to God for the Spirit's power even while he was preaching.

When the Spirit has taught us in the study, the message from the pulpit will be true to the Scriptures and will exalt Jesus Christ. Jesus said of the Spirit, "He will bring glory to me" (John 16:14); and no matter how brilliant or eloquent the preaching may have been, the message wasn't given by the Spirit or delivered in the Spirit if Jesus wasn't glorified. The message will also be balanced: doctrine and duty, privileges and responsibilities, the individual believer and the church as a whole, edification and evangelism, faith and works. Even more, the minister will give the people a balanced diet from various parts of the Scriptures. All Scripture is inspired and "every word" is needed for our spiritual nourishment (Matt. 4:4). The preacher who lingers in favorite books and texts and ignores the total canon of Scripture is a disobedient servant who is robbing the people of needed nourishment and valuable treasure.

Enabling

Most of us are concerned about the power of the Spirit for the preaching of the message. I talked about this in chapter 2. We want our message to come "not simply with words, but also with power, with the Holy Spirit and with deep conviction" (1 Thess. 1:5). But we need to be careful that we don't divorce the power from the Spirit. The Holy Spirit is a person, and whatever power he gives is the result of our relationship to him. If we want his ministry only so we can succeed in preaching a good sermon, then we'll probably be disappointed. That's like the groom saying to the bride, "I take thee as my lawfully wedded cook," or the bride to the groom, "I take thee as my lawfully wedded maintenance man."

The Spirit's ministry to his servants is not à la carte. If we want the fullness of the Spirit for our preaching, we must cultivate a mature relationship to the Spirit in every aspect of his person and work and in every area of our work. I have no right to ask the Holy Spirit to empower me to preach a message that he didn't help me prepare and that I haven't obeyed in my own life. To ignore the Spirit's ministry all week and then implore him for help on Sunday morning is coming dangerously close to tempting the Lord.

It's interesting to read books about the person and work of the Spirit and discover "five steps to the Spirit's fullness" or "ten steps to the Spirit's power." Which is it? "The wind blows wherever it pleases" (John 3:8); so it's dangerous for one believer to assume that his or her experience must be duplicated in the lives of others. One thing is certain: The Spirit is ready to empower and use all who are thirsty for God and want to glorify Christ and bear witness to him. Christian biography makes it clear that whatever process leads to the crisis of fullness is between the believer and God and no two experiences are the same.

God fills clean, available vessels that humbly want to be used for his glory. God commands us to be filled with the Spirit (Eph. 5:18), and his commandments are still his enablements. How can we tell if we're filled with the Spirit? According to Paul, the Spirit-filled believer is joyful (v. 19), thankful (v. 20), and submissive (v. 21), and this submission must be demonstrated first in our homes.

The Power of the Word of God

Not only must we be filled with the Spirit of God, but we must also be filled with the Word of God: "Let the word of Christ dwell in you richly"(Col. 3:16). Since the pronoun *you* is plural, Paul is describing the enrichment of the church by the Word as it is declared and received in the local assembly. Some churches are rich in tradition but poverty-stricken when it comes to the Word. Note that the same characteristics of believers in Ephesians 5 also describe churches that are filled with the Word: They are joyful (v. 16b), thankful (vv.16c–17), and submissive (vv. 18–25). The Spirit of God uses the Word of God to accomplish his purposes. He doesn't work in a vacuum.

It's dangerous to seek the fullness of the Spirit apart from the fullness of the Word, for the Spirit wrote the Word and the Word reveals Christ. The Spirit doesn't empower us so we can be exceptional saints and successful preachers but so that we can obey his Word and manifest Jesus Christ. Any "experience" of the Holy Spirit that ignores or contradicts the Scriptures should be immediately suspect, for it's possible to be fooled by the spirits when we think we're filled with the Spirit. At the same time, it's dangerous to study the Bible apart from experiencing the fullness of the Spirit, because we need the Spirit's power if we're going to practice what we learn. The mark of true Bible study isn't a big head; it's a burning heart and an obedient will.

As we study and preach, we must yield to the Word and believe in its power, first in our own lives and then in the lives of others. The Word is still "living and active"(Heb. 4:12) and accomplishes God's purposes on this earth and in the lives of his people.

The Power of a Praying Church

When you read the Book of Acts, you soon discover that Dr. Luke had several purposes in mind when he wrote it. For one thing, Acts describes the geographical expansion of the church as summarized in 1:8— Jerusalem and all Judea (chs. 1–7), Samaria (ch. 8), and to the end of the earth (chs. 9–28). Luke also reports the numerical growth of the church, beginning with the three thousand converted on the Day of Pentecost (2:41) and ending with Paul's remarkable ministry at Ephesus that reached all Asia Minor (19:20).[1] But Luke also explains the secret behind this incredible expansion and multiplication, for there are at least thirty-five references in Acts to individuals or congregations at prayer.[2]

Blessed are those pastors whose ministry is faithfully supported in prayer by their people! A praying congregation believes that God's power still works today and they assemble, expecting the Holy Spirit to work. In my own itinerant ministry, it's been refreshing in church after church to have groups of laymen lay hands on me and pray earnestly for God's help, and then stay together during the entire service, interceding for God's blessing. Some churches now have a pastor of prayer on staff, or a prayer team, just to encourage the congregation to be a praying people. Throughout the week they see to it that various groups meet to pray and are kept informed of special needs. Here and there you find congregations that have twenty-four-hour prayer meetings, with the members signing up to intercede during a specific hour; and we're also hearing more and more about churches scheduling regular prayer retreats.

The best way to "rewire the pulpit" is to get the people praying! This takes time, and the enemy fights our endeavors and never stops, but we must grow a praying church. When the church is made up of praying people, the preacher can sense it in the study, during his personal pastoral ministry, and especially in the pulpit when he proclaims the Word. "My house will be called a house of prayer," said Jesus, quoting Isaiah the prophet (Matt. 21:13; Isa. 56:7); and when it's a house of prayer, it will also be a house of Spirit-empowered preaching.

Let's teach our people to ask God to give us wisdom and insight as we study the Word, compassion and courage as we prepare the message, and clarity and boldness as we declare the truth from the pulpit. They should pray that we will have the time needed to devote ourselves to the Word of God and prayer (Acts 6:4) and the guidance of the Spirit as we seek the mind of the Lord for the sermon. If we teach our people to pray, then they will also be praying as they assemble for worship and as they listen to the message; and the Lord will work.

The Power of Godly Character

I've pointed out earlier that ministry isn't what we *do* so much as what we *are*.[3] Gifts and abilities are certainly important, but godly character is essential. If preachers and teachers are not seriously striving to be men and women of God, then the Spirit will be grieved and the power diminished and eventually removed. Samson the judge and Saul the king both illustrate this truth. Although the Lord gave each of them a measure of public success, both were disobedient to God and lost the power and blessing of God. The Lord took his Spirit from King Saul (1 Sam. 16:14) and his power from Samson (Judg. 16:18–20), and both had tragic deaths.

The words of Robert Murray M'Cheyne are as true today as when he wrote them in 1840:

> Remember you are God's sword—His instrument—I trust a chosen vessel unto Him to bear His name. In great measure, according to the purity and perfections of the instrument will be the success. It is not great talents God blesses so much as great likeness to Jesus. A holy minister is an awful weapon in the hand of God.[4]

Richard Baxter put it this way nearly two hundred years before:

> O, my brethren, all your preaching and persuading of others will be but dreaming and vile hypocrisy, 'til the work be thoroughly done upon your own hearts.[5]

Amen and amen!

We Preach the Message God Gives Us

> Go to the great city of Nineveh and proclaim to it the message I give you.
>
> The Lord to Jonah
> Jonah 3:1

As far as the record is concerned, the one thing commendable about the prophet Jonah is that he preached the message God gave him, even if he did it reluctantly and with resentment in his heart. But in preaching God's appointed message, Jonah was only following in the train of the prophets before him, for it was one of the marks of true prophets of God that they could honestly declare, "Thus says the Lord!" Unlike the false prophets, who had to dream up their sermons or steal them (Jer. 23:25–32), true prophets had God's message burning in their hearts and they declared it fearlessly in the name of the Lord.

But the prophets and apostles had one advantage we preachers don't have today: They received their messages *immediately* from God, while we receive our messages *mediately* as the Spirit illuminates the Scriptures. One of the special concerns of preachers is that they have the insight week by week to discern just what the Lord wants them to say. The world is asking, "What shall we eat? What shall we drink?" while the preachers are asking, "What shall we preach?"

Guidance

For general guidance in finding the right text, we should pray for God's direction and ask ourselves three questions: (1) What has the Lord been saying to my own heart from his Word? (2) What are the needs of the people? and (3) What truths in Scripture have excited me lately? These questions are important whether our practice is to select a different text each week or to preach an expository series. While each biblical passage has but one interpretation, each passage can yield more than one message and application, and that's where our problems begin.

The first question presupposes a vital devotional life and assumes we spend time daily in the Word and prayer. The work that we do flows out of the life that we live, and the most important part of our life is the part that only God sees. If God isn't speaking *to* me, how can he speak *through* me to others? We aren't reservoirs that pump out sermons; we're channels through whom the water of life can flow. Andrew Bonar said of his friend Robert Murray M'Cheyne, "From the first he fed others by what he himself was feeding upon. His preaching was in a manner the development of his soul's experience. It was a giving out of the inward life."[1]

The second question presupposes pastoral work, a subject we considered in chapter 4. If the ministry from the pulpit is so generic that it could be moved to another church and not miss a beat, then there's something wrong with the ministry. I know that "people are people" and "churches are churches" but I've done enough itinerant work to know that it's difficult to preach week after week to strangers. When preachers turn the sanctuary into a lecture hall and pour out exegetical material week after week, oblivious to the needs of their people, we have truly reached a new low in ministry. In caring for the flock, shepherds can often hear the voice of God sharing the burden of next Sunday's sermon.

The third question presupposes a preacher who studies and dares to pioneer new areas of biblical truth. He isn't fascinated by the fads or captivated by the latest theories. Like Isaac, he digs again the old wells but also digs some new wells (Genesis 26). The preacher who is growing in his knowledge of God and his Word will discover the excitement of sharing truth with the congregation. The important thing is that preachers give themselves time to assimilate the new truths God gives them, integrate them into their theological structure, and activate them in their daily lives. "Test everything. Hold on to the good" (1 Thess. 5:21). After all, what we think is new truth may turn out to be ancient lies with new names.

The Expository Series

The easiest solution to the problem of what to preach, but not the only one, is to preach series of sermons, either expositions of books of the Bible or thematic messages based on biblical truth. There are several advantages to this approach. For one thing, you won't be spending most of the week searching for something to preach. You can work ahead because you know where you're going. However, it's unwise to announce any series, expository or thematic, until you've determined the aim and scope of the messages and have the material well in hand. Early in my ministry I announced a series on Exodus that was no sooner launched than it had to be aborted, much to my embarrassment. I recall a series on the Christian home that I bravely carried to completion but should have stopped after the second sermon. G. Campbell Morgan claimed that he read a book of the Bible forty to fifty times before he analyzed it and prepared his messages or lectures.[2] There's a challenge for you!

Another advantage to the expository series is that you have to preach what's on the page, so nobody can accuse you of painting a target on their back and deliberately singling out their sins. Continuous exposition forces us to deal with topics that are controversial, personal, and difficult, but that's the way both preachers and congregations grow. A third advantage is that you give the people an intelligent overview of various Bible books while at the same time applying the message in a pastoral way. Many people know isolated verses and chapters in Scripture but don't see books as a whole or the Bible as a whole, and expository messages help to give them a more comprehensive view of Scripture.

However, the expository series has its drawbacks, none of which is lethal, but you need to know them. If the series is too long, both you and the congregation may tire of it; so it's wise to interrupt it occasionally to give some balance to the diet. The attention span of the people may be short, so keep in mind that everybody enjoys variety. If the Lord lays a special message on your heart, interrupt the series and preach the preaching God gives you. Keep your eye on the calendar and recognize special seasons, especially Lent and Advent. Sometimes you can work a special-day emphasis into the series and not have to interrupt it, but be sure you don't distort the passage just to make it fit the occasion. And as you enjoy studying the Word and preaching through a book, don't be blind to the special needs that may arise in the church.

As I pointed out in chapter 5, we must recognize the fact that some preachers aren't made for expository preaching and prefer to preach week by week whatever texts God puts on their heart. Charles Spurgeon rarely preached sermon series but he did give popular brief expositions of successive books of the Bible as a part of the regular worship services that related to his sermons. At First Baptist Church, Dallas, Texas, George W. Truett preached the Scriptures textually but didn't preach straight through entire books of the Bible, while his successor W. A. Criswell expounded Scripture book by book. In our own day, Charles Swindoll, James Montgomery Boice, John MacArthur, and the late J. Vernon McGee, among others, have all majored on biblical exposition.

Another factor to consider is the importance of making each message separate and distinctive, though part of a larger series. Not everybody gets to hear every message in the series, and many godly people don't remember everything they hear from the pulpit. The preacher is in trouble if he opens his sermon with, "Now, you'll recall three weeks ago when we started this chapter . . ." The listeners who weren't in the congregation three weeks before may conclude that they won't be able to understand the sermon that day, so they'll tune you out. The people who were there but don't recall what they heard three weeks before may do the same thing! If the sermon text can't stand on it's own two feet, the previous texts may have been either too long or too short.

The expositor must also be sure to prepare structured sermons and not simply study the passage and give a running commentary, what our British friends call a "Bible reading." Even in the finest congregations, there are listeners who need "pegs" to hang their thoughts on, or—to change the image—"handles" by which they can pick up the message and carry it home. The main points of the message are the "pegs" and "handles" many listeners need, but if all we do is saunter from verse to verse without giving definite form to the message, they'll have nothing to get their hands on. Some of my students have pointed to G. Campbell Morgan and H. A. Ironside as successful expositors who preached verse by verse and didn't major on outlines, but if you read their expositions, you'll discover that they were organized and gave their congregations definite markers along the journey. They knew where they were going and how to get there.

A study of church history reveals that God has often used expository preaching to win the lost, edify the saints, and bring revival to the church; but we all must decide before God what gifts we have and how God wants us to use them.

The Thematic Series

It's possible to get too much of a good thing, and variety in our preaching is important. Besides, there are times when the saints need to hear what the Bible has to say about certain topics that are important to the health and safety of the church. However, I don't recommend a steady diet of topical sermons. For one thing, you eventually run out of topics, and it's easy to use all your best material in one sermon. If you're not careful, you may become trendy and start substituting your own ideas for biblical theology. The short topical series can be sandwiched between the longer expository series or dropped in when you've decided the people need a change.

We can combine topical messages with expository preaching by taking our biblical material from passages dealing with that theme.[3] This is a much better approach than merely "proof-texting" the sermon points. One of the most satisfying topical series I ever preached was on the problem of human suffering, but I focused on key passages in Scripture such as Luke 13:1–9; 1 Peter 1:1–9; the Book of Job; Romans 5:1–11; 8:18–23; 2 Corinthians 1:3–11; 12:1–10. This gave me opportunity to explain a subject while at the same time expounding the Word.[4]

In selecting your themes, keep in mind that your congregation is made up of people of all ages who are at various stages of spiritual development; and the larger the congregation, the broader the appeal of the series must be. Topics like "Living with Teenagers" are best discussed in a Sunday school class, but "Staying Whole in a Broken World" is a theme that touches everybody. If you get an idea for a series, start a file and add to it as the excitement grows. Some of your material will end up in the wastebasket, but enough will remain to form the basis for a series of messages that can help your people.

Biographical series are always in order.[5] In fact biographical preaching is especially effective because, if done well, it combines narrative, theology, and practical application in an interesting way. The Bible is a book of biographies, and if you're honest, it's very easy to meet yourself in the Bible.[6] The Bible is a rich treasury of spiritual wealth in which the creative preacher will see endless possibilities for sermon series that combine popular appeal with biblical exposition.

Danger Ahead

We don't want to tempt the Lord or grieve the Spirit by planning so far ahead that there's no opportunity for the Spirit to prepare the preacher and the people for what he wants to say to the church. One famous preacher handed the church organist his preaching schedule *for the entire year* and proceeded to follow it! Of course, he had many years of pulpit experience to draw on, but even so, he faced the danger of his ministry becoming mechanical. The feeling of security we get when we develop a long-range sermon schedule may rob us of the feeling of helplessness we need if we're going to preach with the blessing of God. Even with our long-range planning, without Christ we can do nothing

On the other hand, there's also the danger I've already alluded to of announcing a series that we're not yet prepared to preach. Premature announcements are usually followed by immature messages, because "suddenness leads to shallowness" as the old adage puts it. We must give ourselves time to think through the series theme, see how it applies to the church, and gather and digest the relevant material.

Preaching the "Christian Year"

The people of Israel had their "religious calendar" in Leviticus 23 and each year celebrated a series of special events that reminded them of what the Lord had graciously done for them. The church has its "Christian Year" that commemorates the key events in salvation history, and it's found in the lectionary. Many pastors have found it challenging and rewarding to use a lectionary for the selection of their weekly preaching texts. It offers them several related passages each week and they may select the texts they feel the Lord would have them preach. If anyone argues that the lectionary is a bit too "high church," I reply that it's simply a collection of Scripture passages that takes us through salvation history, what Dorothy Sayers called "the greatest drama ever staged."[7] In the course of one year, it enables the congregation to focus on the life and work of Christ and discover afresh what these events mean to the life and work of the church today.

There are several advantages to using the lectionary. For one thing, it encourages the preacher to consider texts that may be unfamiliar and difficult, a way both preachers and congregations grow spiritually. Using the lectionary also gives continuity to the preaching so that we don't run from Dan to Beersheba in our preaching. Phillips Brooks described these nomadic preachers like this:

> You never begin at the beginning and proceed step by step to the end of any course of orderly instruction. You float over the whole sea of truth, and plunge here and there, like a gull, on any subject that either suits your mood, or that some casual and superficial intercourse with people makes you conceive to be required by a popular need. No other instruction ever was given so.[8]

By preaching through the Christian Year, we can give our people a coherent picture of God's great and gracious plan of redemption and we do it from texts that may be new to them. We cover the basics, the essentials of the Christian faith, and we do it in a systematic way.

Isn't that a good way to instruct people? Of course, this doesn't mean we must slavishly follow the lectionary. It's there as a compass to guide us and not as a road map to determine our every step. In my own ministry, I focused primarily on the exposition of Bible books but I kept my eye on the Christian calendar and helped the church celebrate the great events of salvation history. I tried not to keep an expository series going too long and when there was a natural break in the book, or the calendar called for it, I dropped in a short thematic series.

From Holy Days to Holidays

Most preachers have no problem preaching the great days of the church calendar, but when it comes to secular and patriotic holidays, they wonder what to do. How do we celebrate Mother's Day and Father's Day, Presidents' Day, Veterans Day, and the host of other special days that we see on the calendar? Do we have to preach a sermon commemorating the event? Over the years many churches have changed their approach and recognized the day early in the service, perhaps with a special litany, and then left the preacher free to give whatever message was on his heart.

If you feel led to preach a sermon related to the day, avoid the sentimental and the political and major on the spiritual and the practical. "I never go to church on Father's Day or Mother's Day," a church elder once told me. When I asked him why, he explained, "Because on Mother's Day, our preacher blesses the mothers, and on Father's Day, he bashes the fathers." He might have added that on patriotic holidays, too many preachers become amateur statesmen and tell politicians (who aren't in the congregation) what they ought to do to make the country better.

If you must preach a special-day sermon, the wisest approach is to focus on a central truth related to that day, tie it to a biblical text, and preach the text. There are both good and bad fathers and mothers in the Bible, as well as good and bad rulers and citizens. Our goal is to help people become good Christians, because good Christians should be good spouses, parents, and citizens. In his excellent book of special-day sermons, Clovis Chappell has a sermon on "The Cynic's New Year" with Ecclesiastes 1:9 as the text; and for his Father's Day message, his text was David's lament in 2 Samuel 18:33. One Labor Day Sunday, I preached on "Christ the Carpenter" and one Independence Day, I expounded Romans 13 and spoke on "The Ministry of Being a Good Citizen." We know that these special days are coming, so there's no reason for our not doing our homework well in advance and being prepared. We must use our sanctified imagination, focus on that central truth, relate it to the Christian gospel, and we will have our message.[9]

On December 7, 1941, Peter Marshall was scheduled to preach to the December graduating class of midshipmen at the Naval Academy at Annapolis, and his topic had been announced. But during the previous week, he had the growing feeling that he should change his text to James 4:14, "For what is your life? It is even a vapour, that appeareth for a little time, and then vanisheth away" (KJV). Reluctantly, he followed the leading of his heart and preached from that text. As he drove home that afternoon, he learned why he had preached that message: It was announced over the car radio that Pearl Harbor had been attacked and the United States was at war. The men he had addressed would soon be risking their lives in strange waters, and some of them would die.[10]

Preach the message God gives you.

Eleven
We Preach with Imagination

> The human mind is not, as philosophers would have you think, a debating hall, but a picture gallery.
>
> W. Macneile Dixon

A good sermon will contain helpful information and spiritual inspiration, but if it's going to be interesting and have the power to change lives, it must also be the product of creative imagination.[1] We're made in the image of God, and that means we possess the precious gift of imagination. God is infinitely original, but those of us who speak about God can be painfully dull. We have the potential to be creative, however, because imagination is the creative part of the mind that sees possibilities and finds ways to turn them into realities. The book that you're reading and the computer on which it was written both had their beginning in somebody's imagination.

Obstacles

Some very sincere people get nervous when they hear the word *imagination* connected with preaching, and there may be several reasons for this uneasiness. Perhaps they're uncomfortable because they equate "imagination" with "the imaginary" or "fancy," and they remember Paul's stern warning against preaching man-made myths instead of God-given truth (1 Tim. 4:7; 2 Tim. 4:4). But there's a great difference between "imagination" and "the imaginary." Imagination penetrates the real world and helps us better understand reality, while fancy invents an alternate world—Oz, never-never land, Middle Earth—as an attempt either to escape reality or illustrate some aspect of reality.

A second reason for this concern may be familiarity with the beloved Authorized Version of the Bible. For some reason, the translators saw fit to translate eleven different Hebrew and Greek words as "imagination" *and always with an evil connotation.* Who can forget the description of the people who lived in the days of Noah? "And God saw that the wickedness of man was great in the earth, and that every imagination of the thoughts of his heart was only evil continually" (Gen. 6:5). Those of us who have read the Authorized Version since childhood can't help but believe that the imagination is always wicked, which, of course, is not true. Some very good things in this world are the products of creative imagination.

Perhaps one of the main obstacles to an appreciation of the human imagination is the failure of many believers to see the Bible as literature. "Why would anybody want to use the imagination in reading and studying the Bible?" they ask. "Don't we take the Bible literally?" They forget that the Bible, though inspired by God, is also a magnificent piece of literature, containing narrative, poetry, proverbs, parables, and many other literary forms. We don't spiritualize the parts that are obviously literal, but neither do we treat the poetry of the Psalms the same way we treat the doctrinal exposition in Romans 5. We need a sanctified imagination if we hope to study the Bible seriously, with its many images, symbols, and metaphors.[2]

The fourth reason for this negative attitude toward imagination is the emphasis today on analytical preaching. To put it bluntly, many preachers don't preach the Bible the way the Bible is written. They analyze and outline every passage in the same way and fail to distinguish the literary genre of the text they are studying. What the Bible says is of utmost importance, but how the Bible says it is also important. The speakers in the Bible and the writers of Scripture used metaphorical imagery to convey spiritual truth, and to ignore this imagery is the unpardonable sin of exegesis.

Why Imagination Works

If you were to say, "My friend is like a cool wind on a warm day," you'd be using a simile. Similes use *like* and *as* to compare things. But if you said to your friend, "You are a refreshingly cool wind on a hot day," you'd be using a metaphor. Jesus used metaphors when he said "I am the door" and "I am the true vine." Metaphors bring together things that don't belong together and from this union produce something new. This is what happens when a disgusted mother says to her mud-covered child, "You are a pig!" Of course the child isn't really a pig, but that's the way mothers get their messages across.

Metaphor isn't something we do with language; metaphor is the way language works.[3] In fact we use metaphorical language every day and don't usually think about it. The last time you said to somebody, "I just can't swallow that," you were comparing what the person said (ideas) to food. Statements like "That went right over my head" or "I just don't see that" compare ideas to objects that can be thrown or seen. "You sure lost me with that explanation!" compares speaking to leading people down a path. "This discussion just went on a detour" uses the same metaphor.

The Bible was written as literature and uses the various devices of literature to get the message across. ("Get across" is a metaphor, as in throwing a baseball.) This is the way language works, and that's why imagination works. A good metaphor grabs the attention and interest of our listeners and reaches the mind and the heart. It explodes down inside (that's metaphorical) and produces new insights from old truths. The trouble is that we're so accustomed to the metaphorical language of everyday conversation and of the Bible, we pass right over it and fail to receive both the information and the impact of what was said or written.

When the prophet Isaiah wanted to announce the complete defeat and humiliation of the Moabites, he wrote: "Moab will be trampled under him [the Lord] as straw is trampled down in the manure. They will spread out their hands in it, as a swimmer spreads out his hands to swim" (Isa. 25:10–11). Swimming through manure is an image you can see, feel, and smell! Imagine what would happen if I put the following sermon title on the church announcement board for all to see:

"Next Sunday—Swimming through Manure." But that's why God put imagery in the Bible, to get our attention, arouse our interest, and shake us out of our intellectual lethargy.

How Imagination Works

Your Spirit-directed imagination can perform five services for you as you study the Bible and prepare messages.

First, imagination *recognizes* the imagery in the passage. No sane exegete would take literally all of the elements of the description of Jesus Christ given in Revelation 1:12–16 or the picture of Solomon's beloved in Song of Songs chapter 4. As you cultivate sensitivity to biblical imagery, you will easily identify the similes, metaphors, and symbolic objects, persons, and events found in the passage. (If you want to test yourself now, read Isaiah 59 and identify the images.)

Imagination's second ministry is to help us *analyze* these images and discover what they mean. This is important because the same image may mean a different thing in another passage. Satan is compared to a lion (1 Peter 5:8) but so is Jesus Christ (Rev. 5:5), and water for drinking symbolizes the Spirit of God (John 7:37–39), while water for washing symbolizes the Word of God (John 15:3; Eph. 5:25–27). We must ask ourselves, "What is God saying to us in this image?"

Third, imagination *synthesizes* the images in a passage so we can find the "umbrella" that brings them together. The images in a text aren't so many beads strung on a string; they're more like different colors and shapes woven into a tapestry. For example, in Galatians 5 we find a number of vivid images, among them the yoke (v. 1), profit and loss (v. 2), running a race (v. 7), yeast (v. 9), and fruit (vv. 22–23). The theme that holds them together is living by grace and not returning to the Mosaic law. Legalism will bind us like a yoke and destroy our freedom. It will rob us of spiritual blessing, get us into the wrong lane in the Christian race, and spread like yeast, infecting us and the church.

As we study the text, imagination also helps us *crystallize* the message into a succinct proposition or purpose statement that summarizes the sermon: "Christ purchased freedom for us when he died for us on the cross. If we abandon grace and go back to law, think of the losses that we will incur." You don't preach the images and turn them into allegories; you preach the truths revealed in the images. In the Galatians passage, the images tell us that we will lose our freedom in Christ, the riches of God's grace, progress in the will of God (running the race), and purity of life and doctrine (the yeast).

Finally, imagination helps us *organize* the material so that we present it in a way that captures the imagination and interest of the hearers. Paul begins his defense of grace by taking us to the farm (the yoke). Then he brings us to the bank (profit and loss). We go next to the gymnasium where the contestants are running a race. Finally, we go to the bakery and watch the baker put yeast in the dough. Again, we don't preach the pictures; we use them to declare the spiritual truths that they represent. (If you want another test of your ability to recognize and organize images, prepare a sermon on Psalm 130.)

Cultivating Your Imagination

The word *cultivating* is metaphorical and suggests that a healthy imagination is the result of planting the right seeds, nurturing the plants, fertilizing the soil, and knowing when to pick the fruits. Everybody has an imagination and everybody can develop its powers no matter what age he or she may be. Researchers tell us that children spend their early years with rich imaginative powers, but by the time children reach fifth grade, these powers are almost destroyed in the average classroom. One of the greatest destroyers of the imagination is television, while radio drama and printed literature help the imagination develop. When asked whether she preferred watching television or listening to radio stories, a little girl replied, "I prefer radio because the pictures are clearer." Frank Lloyd Wright is said to have called television "chewing gum for the eyes," and it isn't a bad metaphor.

To help develop our imagination we must do as creative people do. Creative people are readers, and they read widely. It's remarkable how many creative people enjoy reading the comics and have a good sense of humor. They also enjoy words and sometimes even read the dictionary. They like to do crossword puzzles and solve cryptograms. They are alert and notice the people, objects, and events in their surroundings. They like to ask questions of life and what it brings them, especially Why? and What if? If you see them staring into space, that's not lethargy; they're thinking and working. When they get ideas, they write them down and drop them into the right file folder. Life for them is an adventure of ideas and a constant encounter with images.

Some people have an imagination like a glacier; it's frozen, moves slowly, and needs to be defrosted. Others, unfortunately, have an imagination like a sewer, and they need to get it cleaned out. But those who have an imagination like a river experience the creative work of the Spirit of God, and everything that river touches springs into life. Don't be afraid to develop your imagination and use it, because the Bible is a book of inspired but imaginative literature.

Packaging the Truth

Turning an analytical outline into a homiletical outline is an exercise in imagination. We ask ourselves, "How can I package this material so that the people get interested in it and can follow the message easily?" An Eastern proverb says, "The great teacher is the one who turns people's ears into eyes so they can see the truth." That's exactly what Jesus did. He used the familiar to build bridges to the unfamiliar, the natural to explain the spiritual. Every farmer was familiar with seeds, but when Jesus said that the Word of God was seed, the farmers started to think about it. The women in the crowd knew all about yeast but they wondered why Jesus said that the kingdom of heaven was like a woman putting yeast into dough.

Psalm 130 has four stanzas and each of them paints a picture.

1. A person crying out for help—vv. 1–2
2. A person seeking forgiveness—vv. 3–4
3. A person waiting for sunrise—vv. 5–6
4. A person (slave?) hoping to be set free—vv. 7–8

The first person is drowning ("Out of the depths"), probably under the waves and billows of sin or sorrow or despair. What's needed is God's mercy. The second person is in court and all the evidence points to "Guilty!" God keeps good records. The third person is watching on the walls for the enemy to arrive and start to besiege the city. If only the sun would come up! The last person is in bondage, wondering if anybody will pay the price for redemption.

What is the overriding theme that ties together these images of drowning, guilt, darkness, and bondage? It's sin (vv. 3 and 8). The sinner is pictured as a person drowning in the sea, a guilty prisoner standing in the courtroom, a night watcher on the walls, and a slave in bondage. The answer to these plights is God's mercy (v. 1), forgiveness (v. 4), and redemption (v. 7). What happens when sinners cry out to God for salvation and put their faith in Jesus Christ?

1. They go from death to life—vv. 1–2
2. They go from guilt to forgiveness—vv. 3–4
3. They go from darkness to light (dawning of a new day)—vv. 5–6
4. They go from bondage to freedom—vv. 7–8

God's Inspired Picture Book

God uses pictures and picture language to teach us his marvelous truth and we're foolish not to make use of these pictures as we expound the Scriptures. He pictures temptation as a beast waiting at the door (Gen. 4:7), a hungry guest we let through the door and feed (2 Sam. 12:1–4), and a womb impregnated by desire and giving birth to sin and death (James 1:13–15).[4] In the Book of Revelation the holy city is a pure bride, but Babylon, the godless world system, is a prostitute. In John 10 Jesus is the sacrificing Good Shepherd, but Satan is a thief and a robber. According to John's Gospel, salvation means experiencing new birth, drinking living water, eating living bread, having our eyes opened to the light, and following the Good Shepherd into the green pastures. And these are but a few of the captivating pictures of salvation found in the Word of God.

"The Christian is the one whose imagination should fly beyond the stars," wrote Francis Schaeffer.[5] At the same time, we should keep our feet firmly planted on the foundation of Christ and the gospel. The combination makes for effective preaching.

Twelve

We Preach to the Occasion

> I believe in using almost any special occasion as an opportunity for preaching the Gospel.
>
> D. Martyn Lloyd-Jones
> *Preaching and Preachers*

Preachers never feel like they have enough time to prepare their messages, but most of us eventually develop a pattern of sermon preparation that works satisfactorily from week to week. We also know that at any time we may be confronted with an occasion that demands a special message, and then we have even less time to get ready. Death doesn't always signal ahead, so funeral services head the list of the unexpected, but they don't exhaust the list. At the last minute, the couple you're preparing for marriage learns that Uncle Hugo is coming to the wedding, so they ask you to preach a sermon or say something convicting at the reception. You may get an invitation to speak at the dedication of a new church sanctuary or perhaps the celebration of a wedding anniversary. I was once asked to give a devotional message for the dedication of a new house, and there have been numerous anniversary celebrations where I was expected to minister the Word. I was even asked to "say something religious" at the dedication of a new high school gymnasium!

I have two pieces of advice that will help you prepare for these unexpected opportunities, and the first is this: *Never allow a good text to slip through your fingers.* Often while preparing a sermon or reading the Bible devotionally, I've heard a text say, "I'm just right for a baccalaureate address"; so I've written down the reference and the sermon idea on a file card and put it in the proper folder. Weeks later, another text may jump out and shout, "Use me at the next ordination service!" and I give it the same careful treatment. When I was in pastoral ministry, I kept a special notebook of ideas for messages to use at funerals and memorial services. Andrew Blackwood called these idea files "the sermonic seed plot," and it's an apt metaphor. You plant the texts, water them occasionally with prayer and meditation, and trust God for the harvest.

My second piece of counsel is that you *tie every "special occasion" message to the Word of God and the heart of the occasion.* When speaking at a fiftieth anniversary reception, you will certainly want to say something personal about the people involved; but after you've done that, you'll want to say something about God's love for these people, his providential leading, and his faithful care. Texts like Psalm 90:1 and 12 come to mind, as well as the testimonies of "senior saints" like Jacob (Genesis 49), Joshua (Josh. 23:14; 24:15), and David (Ps. 37:25).

Now let's consider some of these unexpected challenges.

Funerals and Memorial Services

No pastoral responsibility is more demanding than ministering comfort to people who are shocked and bereaved because of the death of a loved one, especially if that death was very sudden or was a suicide. Particularly painful is the death of a child. On more than one occasion, I've wondered what I would say at the service; but thanks to the "seed plot," the Lord has always been gracious to give me just what I needed.

It's my conviction that the purpose of the funeral message is to exalt Jesus Christ as the adequate answer to every problem. He is the only one who fully understands how we feel and what we need. The funeral or memorial service is not an occasion for complicated theological discussion or debate; it's an opportunity to help heal broken hearts by sharing the promises of God's Word. I once had to sit through a tedious theological explanation of 1 Corinthians 15 that brought us comfort only when it ended. The minister didn't realize that God's people don't live on explanations, they live on promises, and that there's a vast difference between applying the medicine and analyzing the prescription.[1]

Both in content and delivery, the message should be pastoral and deal with one "luminous truth" (the phrase is Andrew Blackwood's) that points to the adequacy of Jesus Christ. As people go through the valley, they can't handle the abstractions of systematic theology but they can see the biblical images that reveal a caring and comforting Savior. In 1 Corinthians 15, when Paul discussed the resurrection, he wrote about seeds and stars and changing clothes (vv. 35–57), images that even grieving people can understand. The message should be brief but not hurried and should appeal to the imagination and the heart. Needless to say, we always declare the gospel in every message. If you have a shepherd's heart and a well-read Bible, the Spirit will lead you to say the right things in the right way.

Don't build the message on obscure and unusual texts or on texts that demand extended explanations. Like children reaching out for their parents' comforting arms, people in sorrow reach out for the familiar promises of God and embrace them afresh. Some ministers have a generic sermon that they use at every funeral they conduct, whether the deceased is a stillborn child or a centenarian; but it's better to tailor the message to the occasion and make it personal. I once attended a funeral during which the name of the deceased wasn't mentioned even once, and it was not a comforting service. Jesus calls his own sheep by name, even after they're dead (John 11:11); and this isn't a difficult example to follow.

My practice was to open the service by quoting Scripture, starting with 1 John 3:1–2, then moving to John 14:1–6; 1 Thessalonians 4:13–18; and Psalm 46. Then I would pray briefly, asking the Father to help us honor the deceased and glorify the Lord Jesus even in our sorrow. If the family requested music and a eulogy, these would follow, and then I would give the message. Unless the deceased was a very well-known person in the church or community and several people had been asked to speak, I tried to limit the service to about thirty minutes, and shorter if possible. The best way to honor the dead is to care for the living.

Next to our own relationship with the Lord, the most important element in ministering to the bereaved is that intangible bond between pastor and people. It's a living link forged over the years as the shepherd and the sheep have walked, worked, and wept together. When that bond is strong, the message will be the right one.

The Wedding Sermon

I usually tried to convince the couple not to interrupt a beautiful marriage ceremony with a sermon, but I didn't always succeed. It's a bit late to be preaching about marriage to the bride and groom; and as for Uncle Hugo, if the total impact of a Christian wedding, planned for God's glory, doesn't reach his heart, then a sermon probably wouldn't reach him either. There are ministers who can turn funerals and weddings into evangelistic meetings and even give invitations, but I'm not yet among them. With the Lord's help, the couple and I would try to make the ceremony itself such a witness to Christ and the gospel that the message of God's love clearly came across. Unbelieving relatives or friends frequently asked me afterwards, "Where did you get that ceremony? It was very touching." When I told them it was adapted from *The Book of Common Prayer* and had been around for decades, they were surprised. But their interest opened the door for further witness, and the Lord brought some of them to himself.

But if the loving couple insists that you preach a wedding sermon, you can take one of two approaches. The easier route is to give a brief message early in the ceremony but not call it a sermon or have it identified as such in the printed wedding program. Keep the message brief and to the point. The more difficult approach is to weave the message throughout the ceremony as though it were a standard part of the liturgy. The most important thing about the wedding sermon is that it not sound like a sermon. The guests must not think that you're preaching over the couple's shoulders and taking potshots at their unconverted family members and friends. If the atmosphere of the service reveals Christian joy and love, the entire ceremony will be a sermon in itself.

Dedicating a New Church Edifice

Few things test the faith, patience, and love of a church family, large or small, like constructing a new building. When people tell me their church is moving into a building program, I usually warn them to add three months to the schedule and 20 percent to the budget; and it's remarkable how accurate my predictions have been. Building programs aren't easy; they usually bring out the best in some people and the worst in others.

So if you're going to help a congregation dedicate a new edifice to the Lord, rejoice with them and focus their hearts on the goodness and grace of God. Don't major on the negative, as though the building committee, the elders, and the membership in general all should go to the altar and get right with God and with one another. Perhaps congregational healing is in order, but the pastor can work on that in the weeks that follow. Our job is to unite the congregation in dedicating to the Lord both the building and the membership. It should be a service that expresses gratitude to God and that leads to a new beginning for his people.

Of course God doesn't dwell in buildings, but families do, and the church is God's family. A building is a tool for the saints to use as they edify one another and work together to evangelize the lost. Most of the work of the church goes on outside the buildings, but God's people need someplace to meet for corporate worship and personal training. A building is also a testimony to the faithfulness of God and the faith of God's people. It should be a "house of prayer for all nations."

According to Isaiah 66:1–2 everything that goes into a church building program ultimately comes from God and we can't take credit for it. The Lord dwells in the hearts of the humble, those who respect his Word. It's good to look around and praise God for all he's done, but it's more important to look within and see if we're a fit dwelling place for the King (Eph. 2:19–22).

In 1 Corinthians 3:9 Paul joins two images of the church: the field and the building. Is he reminding us that the building exists for the field? The purpose of the field is a harvest for God, and the purpose of the building is a holy dwelling for God. Both are important. The field speaks of *quantity* but the building speaks of *quality*. To achieve both takes diligence and hard work. The harvest is the test of our work in the field, but our work on the spiritual building won't be revealed until the judgment. Churches build physical buildings with the finest materials but try to construct the spiritual building with "wood, hay or straw" (v. 12). How foolish!

A dedication message should focus on some aspect of the dynamics of church life as described in the Book of Acts and commanded in the Epistles. Often at a dedication service, the contractor or architect gives a key to the chairman of the trustees, a symbolic gesture, of course, but a very meaningful one. Why build a building if nobody can open the door and go in or go out? As I said in chapter 9, the church in Acts 1 is "The Church of the Closed Door." I once preached on that theme, tracing it through the Book of Acts. In chapter 1 of Acts the doors are closed and the believers are doing what most churches do today: meeting together, praying, electing officers, and studying the Scriptures. But nobody is being reached and changed because the believers are waiting for the Spirit to come. When the Spirit comes, the doors are opened and the message of the gospel is proclaimed with power (ch. 2). The Holy Spirit is the one who has the key and we must depend on him. The rest of the Book of Acts is a record of God opening doors and the enemy trying to close them.

What If?

Conscientious preachers frequently ask themselves questions about possible ministry opportunities and then try to answer them. *What if I were asked to speak at a PTA Christmas party? What if I were invited to address the local Bar Association? If one of our church lads achieved Eagle Scout status and asked me to speak at the service, what would I say? How would I bring the gospel to a local veterans' group and what text would I use?*

Sometimes these intuitions actually turn into invitations, and that's when we learn to appreciate our sermonic seed plot. And don't overlook the messages you've already prepared, because it's possible to take the basic material of a sermon and adapt it effectively to a new situation. This is where the "art of preaching" becomes important, for the true artist knows how to transform the old into the new without distorting either one.

It's proper to *adapt* a message to a new congregation, but it's wrong to *accommodate* a message to any congregation. You adapt a message when you adjust the content and delivery so that the message will become more meaningful to the listeners, but you accommodate a message when you change it to become more acceptable to the listeners. The first is sincere communication with the Word in control; the second is dishonest manipulation with the audience in control. The faithful preacher pleases God by working hard to get the message across, while the unfaithful preacher tries only to please his hearers by leaving out anything that might be offensive to them. In 1 Thessalonians 2:1–5, Paul had something to say about the sin of distorting and diluting God's truth.

We Preach as Part
of a Great Tradition

> Those who cannot remember the past are con-
> demned to repeat it.
>
> George Santayana
> The Life of Reason

Artists, writers, and composers get acquainted with the lives and works of other artists, writers, and composers who came before them, and there's no reason why preachers shouldn't follow this good example. I once taught an elective course on the history of preaching and was pleased that a dozen students showed up. However, I quickly discovered that they didn't recognize the names of even the most distinguished preachers of the past. When I mentioned some notable nineteenth-century pulpiteers, I drew a blank, except for one student who recognized Phillips Brooks as the author of "O Little Town of Bethlehem."

Those of us who preach God's Word are privileged to be part of an ancient calling and tradition that goes all the way back to Enoch and Noah (Gen. 5:18–24;

Jude 14–15; 2 Peter 2:5). To cut ourselves off from this heritage is folly. When it comes to homiletical history, there's an incredible wealth of information and inspiration just waiting to be mined and minted by each new generation; but some of today's ministers need to be motivated to locate the mines and start digging. There are also some newer books on homiletics that are opening up rich veins that prove promising, and we need to pay attention to them as well. Whether we look back or look ahead, the quest for more effective preaching should never end.

What We Can Learn

From my own experience, I can report that the many hours I've invested reading and rereading the sermons, biographies, and autobiographies of the prominent preachers of the past and present have enriched my life tremendously and have also enriched my ministry. For one thing, I've learned that God chooses and uses people of various personalities and abilities and even different theological persuasions. That's encouraging. The Lord doesn't expect me to be like Charles Spurgeon or G. Campbell Morgan or Bishop Westcott or any current preacher whose smiling photograph greets me at the Christian bookstore. God wants me to be myself—my *best* self—and to serve the best I can as I use the gifts and opportunities he gives me. After all, being myself is the real secret of originality. Meeting the distinguished preachers of the past and learning how the Lord worked in and through their lives can help me better understand how God works in Christian ministry today and makes his ministers what they ought to be.

But nobody lives in a vacuum. My friendship with these distinguished servants of God has also introduced me to the times in which they lived, and this has opened up new horizons of study and thought. Each age in history has its own peculiar challenges, issues, and critical events, and seeing my preacher friends in their historical setting has helped me better understand why they thought, preached, and ministered as they did. As I mentioned earlier in this book, the younger preachers today may need to catch up on the past, and when they do, they'll discover how remarkably contemporary it is. There's nothing new under the sun or in the pulpit.

One of the best ways to get acquainted with history in general and church history in particular is to read biography and autobiography. My long fascination with the Victorian Era began with an interest in the eminent preachers of the nineteenth century, of whom there were many. The Oxford Movement then got my attention and I began to investigate the ministries of Keble, Pusey, and Newman, and this led to a special interest in Cardinal Newman. Out of this grew a study of Anglican theology and liturgy and then an investigation of Christian worship in general. Once you get started on one of these biographical bypaths, you never know where it will lead. But you can be sure that if you courageously follow the trail, it will lead you to wider views of God's work in this world as well as greater appreciation for the people who came before you. You'll also be surprised to discover that you have more in common with the people and communions you disagree with, and that always helps.

My suggestion is that you select one or two preachers who really interest you and learn all you can from them and about them. Begin with autobiographies and find out what these people said about themselves, and then read what others said about them. Read their sermons and how others evaluated their preaching. Follow whatever interests you—the people in their lives you've never heard of before or the theological issues of that time—and lay hold of the principles and lessons that apply to your life and ministry today. "The one thing we learn from history is that we don't learn from history," said Hegel,[1] but that doesn't have to be true for us as we study the history of preaching.

To get started, add to your library a set of *A Treasury of Great Preaching*, edited by Clyde E. Fant Jr. and William M. Pinson Jr. (Nelson, 1995), originally published by Word as *20 Centuries of Great Preaching*. This encyclopedia of preachers and preaching begins with Jesus and the apostles and takes you across the centuries to Billy Graham and Martin Luther King Jr. A biographical essay introduces each preacher, followed by a study of his preaching and a selection of his sermons. The bibliographies will tell you which books to read for further study of the ninety-five preachers included in the set.

For a comprehensive one-volume approach to the history of preaching, *The Company of Preachers* by David L. Larsen (Kregel, 1998) is your best choice. The book begins with the Old Testament prophets and takes you up to A. W. Tozer, who died in 1963. If you can locate a used set of the three-volume *A History of Preaching in Britain and America* by F. R. Webber (Milwaukee: Northwestern Publishing, 1952, 1955, 1957), you will have added a treasure to your collection. Webber begins with the preaching of the Celtic church in Great Britain and closes with the preachers of the first half of the twentieth century. His final chapter is on evangelical preaching and sounds the warning that if the pulpit fails to preach evangelical doctrine, the church will weaken and die.

Edwin C. Dargan wrote a two-volume history of preaching that was published in 1905 and 1912, and it covered Continental preaching as well as preaching in Britain and America. He began with the apostolic church and ended with the closing years of the nineteenth century. Baker Book House reprinted these volumes in 1974 along with a third volume written by Ralph G. Turnbull that brought the story up to 1950 and dealt with preaching almost worldwide.

Voices from the Past

It's easy to read printed sermons but it's not always easy to interpret them accurately. For one thing, you can't hear the preacher's voice so you don't know how he spoke when he gave the message you're reading. Another limitation is that you don't know the responses of the congregation. It might have helped today's readers if the stenographers who reported the sermons had added "great laughter" or "loud amens" to the text, but the preachers probably would have disapproved.

But beyond these two hurdles is the fact that almost all printed sermons have been edited for publication, except those that were delivered from manuscripts. Translating the spoken word into the written word isn't easy because words can't fully convey the look on the preacher's face and the tone of his voice. I have a galley proof of Spurgeon's sermon on Hebrews 7:2 and every paragraph has changes in it, even if only the punctuation. I'm not a handwriting expert, but in comparing the writing on the proof with the samples in his autobiography, it appears that the great man himself did the editing; and he, or whoever did the editing, certainly made many changes.[2] During my ministry, I've often had to edit radio messages for publication and I assure you it's easier to write the message from scratch than it is to rework transcriptions. The personality of the preacher comes through with greater power when the transcription is untouched, but not many publishers would print an unedited version of a sermon, and I'm not sure I'd want them to do so.

If you do your homework and learn about the preachers and their times, you'll find that their published sermons will mean more to you; but don't read anybody's sermon as a professional preacher fulfilling an academic assignment. Read the sermon first as a sinner who needs to know more about God and his grace. First get nourishment for your own soul, and leave the academics until later. When you do get around to studying the sermon, here are some questions you might want to ask:[3]

1. Did the introduction get your attention and make you want to continue reading? Was the introduction too long? Too brief?
2. Was the propositional statement clear, concise, and inviting? Was it true to the text or tangential to the text?
3. Were the main points of the sermon simply stated and directly related to the purpose statement? Was there anything artificial about the main points that distracted from the sermon itself?
4. Did the development of the sermon fulfill the promise of the introduction?
5. Did the illustrations contribute to the development?
6. How did the preacher apply the truth to life?
7. Was the sermon vitally related to the text?

8. How did the preacher conclude the message? Was this effective?
9. How did the message declare the gospel of Jesus Christ?
10. What changes would you have made to make the message more effective?

There are numerous one-volume sermon anthologies available. My own *A Treasury of the World's Great Sermons* (Kregel, 1977) will introduce you to one hundred twenty-three eminent preachers. *The Twentieth Century Pulpit,* edited by James W. Cox (Abingdon, 1978), contains sermons by thirty-seven preachers from an exciting variety of callings and theological persuasions. It's not only an excellent collection but it serves as a good companion volume to *The Protestant Pulpit,* edited by Andrew Blackwood (Abingdon, 1947). *The Best Sermons* series covers a wider range of the theological spectrum, but I enjoy reading sermons by preachers who look at God, Christ, and the Bible through spectacles different from my own.

In time you'll find that certain preachers speak to you clearly, while others bore you; but before you reject the others, try to determine why their ministry doesn't move you. Once you've solved that mystery, select one or two preachers who come across with interest and power and study them and their sermons until they've become old friends, and then pick another one to study.

I don't want to urge my own preferences on you, but the preachers whose sermons have most reached my own heart and mind are Charles Haddon Spurgeon, Alexander Whyte, G. Campbell Morgan, Alexander Maclaren, Clarence Macartney, Clovis Chappell, George Morrison, Joseph Parker, F. W. Robertson, J. Wallace Hamilton, Robert Murray M'Cheyne, J. D.

Jones, John Henry Jowett, Phillips Brooks, James S. Stewart, and George W. Truett. If some of your favorite preachers are missing from this list, don't panic. Their absence doesn't mean that one of us is mistaken, but only that we have different interests and tastes. There are some excellent preachers whom I still have to "grow into," and I hope I will before it's too late.

Books on Preaching

Each year I try to read a new book on some aspect of preaching as well as review one I've read before. If you read enough books on homiletics, you'll discover that they fall into three general categories: (1) *classical homiletics,* which may have begun with the publication of Jean Claude's "Essay on the Composition of a Sermon" in 1688[4] and ended somewhere in the middle of the twentieth century; (2) *transition homiletics,* say 1950 to 1975, when we discovered communications theory and literary criticism and began to apply new knowledge to the old techniques; and (3) *contemporary homiletics* (1975–present), which is where we are today, wedding the old and the new and hoping the marriage will give birth to the approach to preaching that will get the job done better today.

I'm not advocating that we abandon the principles of classical homiletics as they apply to the exposition of the Word of God. But I feel that we must not preach in a time warp and think that by imitating the Puritans, Charles Spurgeon, or Billy Sunday we're guaranteed to reach the hearts and minds of people in a new millennium. Each new generation must evaluate the homiletical data and the preaching styles of those who came before, learn from them, and hold to what is good. This doesn't mean we reject the past and automatically embrace every pulpit innovation that comes along. The fact that something is old doesn't mean that it's bad any more than the fact that it's new automatically makes it good. I would no doubt get the attention of the public if I preached in a clown suit but I'm not sure that doing so would make the message better or the communicating easier.

Classical Homiletics

Heading the list is Phillips Brooks's *Lectures on Preaching*, available in many editions, old and new. The Kregel edition is called *The Joy of Preaching*. I've frequently made this book required reading in my preaching classes, knowing some student was bound to ask, "Aren't there any books on preaching more contemporary than 1877?" My answer was always, "Yes, there are, and I recommend you read them; but I still feel that much that's been published on homiletics in America is a footnote to Phillips Brooks." For the most part, the Yale Lectures on Preaching series through 1938 majors on classical homiletics. *Preaching in These Times*, published in 1940, was the beginning of a significant turning point, and later volumes have broadened the scope.[5]

I could list hundreds of titles in the classical category but I'll limit myself to just a few. *The Preacher: His Life and Work* by John Henry Jowett (Harper, 1912) is a part of the Yale Lectures series, as is *Jesus Came Preaching* by George A. Buttrick (Charles Scribner's Sons, 1931). *In the Minister's Workshop* by Halford E. Luccock is still a helpful volume (Abingdon, 1944) and so are the volumes written by Charles W. Koller and Lloyd M. Perry, who were my preaching professors in seminary and to whom I owe an incalculable debt. Baker Book House combined Koller's *Expository Preaching without*

Notes (1962) with his *Sermons Preached without Notes* (1964) into one volume *How to Preach without Notes.* You can learn his homiletical approach and at the same time read the sermons that it helped to produce. Of Perry's many books, I think the *Biblical Sermon Guide* (Baker, 1970) and *Biblical Preaching for Today's World* (Moody, 1973; revised edition, 1990) are the two best; but all of them are helpful.

Other useful volumes in the classical tradition are *Preaching the Good News* by George E. Sweazey (Prentice-Hall, 1976); *Preaching and Preachers* by D. Martyn Lloyd-Jones (Hodder and Stoughton, 1971); and *The Mystery of Preaching* by James Black (Zondervan, 1978). The most helpful survey is *Theories of Preaching*, edited by Richard Lischer (Labyrinth Press, 1987), which is an anthology of forty-eight readings from a wide variety of preachers and scholars.

Transitional Homiletics

Every academic discipline is always experiencing some kind of transition, so *transition* may not be the most accurate word to use. I'm referring to the period from 1950 to perhaps 1975, when preaching in general and expository preaching in particular were under attack, as new theories and methods challenged traditional homiletics. *Design for Preaching* by H. Grady Davis (Fortress, 1958) brought a breath of fresh air and still remains an exciting book to read. Davis's discussions of thoughts, forms, functions, and substance not only introduced new terminology but also shattered some cherished traditions. In 1961 Charles Scribner's Sons published *A New Look at Preaching* by the controversial James A. Pike who took the mercantile approach and made the preacher a salesman. In spite of this nonbiblical metaphor, his little book helped open new trails.

As One without Authority by Fred B. Craddock (Abingdon, 1971) proved to be a provocative book whenever I used it as a class text, because of its emphasis on inductive preaching. Thor Hall's *The Future Shape of Preaching* (Fortress, 1971) put preaching into the context of modern media and urged us to understand and use "religious language" so people know what we're saying. The Yale Lectures for 1979 were given by John R. Claypool and published under the title *The Preaching Event* (Word, 1980). Claypool presents the preacher as reconciler, gift-giver, witness, and nurturer, all of which sound strongly pastoral, but the metaphors also have something to say about preaching. That same year Haddon W. Robinson published *Biblical Preaching* (Baker, 1980), a wise and careful blending of classical homiletics and contemporary thinking.

In *Between Two Worlds* (Eerdmans, 1982), John R. W. Stott sees the preacher as a bridge-builder who, if he expects to span the communications chasm, must know the mind of God revealed in the Bible and the minds of the listeners as seen in contemporary society. Quite a challenge, and he tells us how to meet it. *Heralds to a New Age,* edited by Don M. Aycock (Brethren Press, 1985), is a collection of essays on various aspects of preaching, written by specialists who are asking, "What will preaching be like in the twenty-first century?" Some of the chapters are helpful but tame. Seward Hiltner, however, writes about the pastor as a clown in the circus, and William E. Hull gives an expository essay based on 2 Corinthians 4:5 that blows away some dust. Reuel L. Howe deals with communication barriers and Earl H. Furgeson warns us about abstractions in preaching.

The biggest and most disturbing of all the transitional books was *Homiletic: Moves and Structures* by David Buttrick (Fortress, 1987) in which the author applied phenomenology to preaching. He defined his purpose as discovering "how sermons happen in consciousness," the consciousness of both the preacher and the listener. In other words, preachers don't just tell people what to do; they help the people *see* what they should do. Preaching is both discovery and experience and not just religious education. Finally, Bryan Chapell's *Christ-Centered Preaching* (Baker, 1994) does some new things with old forms and helps us bring excitement to expository preaching.

Contemporary Homiletics

I'm speaking here, not about copyright dates, but about the concepts found in the books. *Preaching for Today* by Clyde E. Fant Jr. (Harper and Row, 1975) emphasizes what the author calls "incarnational preaching." It's an attempt to bring together the two "heretical" extremes of preaching: being too preoccupied with the historical and the theological or being too preoccupied with the contemporary and the human. In other words, preaching in the present tense.

If you haven't yet discovered the writings of Frederick Buechner (pronounced BEEK-ner), you are in for a treat. *Telling the Truth: The Gospel as Tragedy, Comedy and Fairy Tale* was published in 1977 by Harper and Row and constitutes Buechner's contribution to the Yale Lectures series. This slim book reveals him as both novelist and preacher as he examines the literature of the Bible and shows how it relates to our story-conscious world. To read some of Buechner's sermons, secure *The Magnificent Defeat* (Seabury, 1983). If you were trained in the forties and fifties and want to become sensitive to the contemporary mindset, a good dose of Buechner would help. In a similar vein is *The Homiletical Plot* by Eugene L. Lowry (John Knox, 1980), an excellent introduction to narrative preaching.

Calvin Miller's *Spirit, Word and Story* (Word, 1989; Baker, 1996) and *Marketplace Preaching* (Baker, 1996) both focus on the sermon as story and the need to understand the thinking of our media-influenced congregations. *The Sermon as Symphony* by Mike Graves (Judson, 1997) examines ten literary forms in the New Testament and illustrates with contemporary sermons how these texts can be preached. In a day when a great deal is said about seeker-sensitive services, the author pleads for "form-sensitive sermons." The well-known theologian Thomas F. Torrance helps us confront today's scientific mind with *Preaching Christ Today* (Eerdmans, 1994), two addresses in which Dr. Torrance shows that the preacher and the scientist have more in common than we might imagine.

Don't impulsively accept everything you find in any homiletics book, including this one, and don't imitate all that you read in every sermon without first testing everything by the Word and careful practice. Don't follow every fad, but at the same time don't close your ears and eyes to what the Spirit is saying to the church and doing among his people. You are part of a great tradition and you want to do your best. Who knows? Some eager homiletics class may be reading and studying your sermons one day in the future!

Notes

Chapter 1: We Preach

1. John A. Broadus, *A Treatise on the Preparation and Delivery of Sermons* (New York: A. C. Armstrong, 1897), 17. Though published a century ago, this is a basic text on homiletics and deserves to be read today. In 1944 Harper Brothers published a revised edition edited by Jesse B. Weatherspoon.

2. Phillips Brooks, *Lectures on Preaching* (Grand Rapids: Baker, 1969), 3–4. Most of what has been published on homiletics in America since 1877 is an expansion of what Brooks said in these lectures. Each time I read them, I'm struck with how contemporary and fundamental they are.

3. John Watson, *The Cure of Souls* (London: Hodder and Stoughton, 1896), 3.

4. D. Martyn Lloyd-Jones, *Preaching and Preachers* (London: Hodder and Stoughton, 1971), 9.

5. John R. W. Stott, *Between Two Worlds: The Art of Preaching in the Twentieth Century* (Grand Rapids: Eerdmans, 1982), 16. Stott uses "bridge-building" as his guiding metaphor for preaching. In his autobiography, *The Living of These Days,* Harry Emerson Fosdick used the

same metaphor: "A good sermon is an engineering operation by which a chasm is bridged so that spiritual goods on one side—'the unsearchable riches of Christ'—are actually transported into personal lives on the other" (New York: Harper, 1956), 99.

6. Bryan Chapell, *Christ-Centered Preaching* (Grand Rapids: Baker, 1994), 17. Robert G. Rayburn was the founding president of Covenant Theological Seminary and served as professor of homiletics from 1956 to 1984.

7. In the parable of the sower (Matt. 13:1–9, 18–23), the seed is the Word of God; but in the parable of the weeds (Matt. 13:24–30, 36–43), the good seed represented the children of the kingdom. The Word has become flesh.

8. Brooks's definition appears in *Lectures on Preaching:* "Preaching is the communication of truth by man to man" (p. 5).

9. Jacques Ellul, *The Humiliation of the Word,* trans. Joyce Main Hanks (Grand Rapids: Eerdmans, 1985), 109. I recommend this book to the serious student of preaching. Ellul discusses the differences that exist between the "image" culture and the "word" culture and how these differences relate to the matter of sharing the Word of God with a lost world.

10. G. A. Barbour, *The Life of Alexander Whyte* (London: Hodder and Stoughton, 1923), 307–8.

Chapter 2: We Preach the Scriptures

1. Quoted in Stott, *Between Two Worlds,* 103.

2. Spurgeon, *The Metropolitan Tabernacle Pulpit,* vol. 27 (Pasadena, Tex.: Pilgrim, 1984), 42.

3. Stanley and Patricia Gundry, *The Wit and Wisdom of D. L. Moody* (Chicago: Moody, 1974), 40.

Chapter 3: We Preach Christ

1. Spurgeon, *The Metropolitan Tabernacle Pulpit,* vol. 13, 489.
2. The difference between the "milk" and the "meat" in Heb. 5:9–6:3 has to do with the distinction between Christ's finished work on earth ("milk") and his present unfinished work in heaven ("meat"). The writer had discussed the basic principles of his earthly work and wanted to move into a discussion of his present ministry in heaven as high priest "according to the order of Melchizedek," but the spiritual dullness of his readers made this difficult.
3. Quoted in Ralph G. Turnbull, *A Minister's Obstacles* (New York: Revell, 1946), 45.
4. Brooks, *Lectures on Preaching,* 46–47.
5. Spurgeon, *Metropolitan Tabernacle Pulpit,* vol. 14, 467.

Chapter 4: We Preach to Real People

1. Henry David Thoreau, *Walden* (Princeton, N.J.: Princeton University Press, 1971), 8.
2. James Boswell, *The Life of Samuel Johnson,* vol. 1 (London: James Dent, 1973), 163.
3. Sad to say, Arthur Godfrey violated his own principle of the personal touch when on October 19, 1953, he fired singer Julius LaRosa while the broadcast was being aired. It didn't help Godfrey's ratings.
4. Note in this verse that Paul was right in his message ("error"), his motives, and his methods. People who say, "I don't care what your methods are so long as your message is right" wouldn't get along well with the apostle. There are some methods of ministry that are unworthy of the message we preach and the Christ we represent.
5. See Ashley Montagu and Floyd Matson, *The De-humanization of Man* (New York: McGraw-Hill, 1983), and

Martin L. Gross, *The Psychological Society* (New York: Random House, 1978).

6. George Orwell, *Nineteen Eighty-Four*, part 3, chapter 3.

7. See Hugh Evan Hopkins, *Charles Simeon of Cambridge* (Grand Rapids: Eerdmans, 1977), 63–65.

8. Henri J. M. Nouwen, *With Open Hands* (Notre Dame, Ind.: Ave Maria Press, 1972), 7.

9. Boswell, *The Life of Samuel Johnson*, 288.

10. *George Whitefield's Journals* (London: Banner of Truth Trust, 1965), 79.

11. Brooks, *Lectures on Preaching*, 77.

12. Thoreau, *Walden*, 4.

13. W. Robertson Nicoll, *People and Books* (New York: George H. Doran, n.d.), 106–7.

14. Fosdick, *The Living of These Days*, 99. "Only the preacher proceeds still upon the idea that folk come to church desperately anxious to discover what happened to the Jebusites" (p. 92).

15. John Henry Jowett, *The Minister: His Life and Work* (New York: Harper, 1912), 136–37.

16. Cited in Robert B. Downs, *Books That Changed the World* (New York: New American Library, 1956), 129.

17. See Elton Trueblood, *The Humor of Jesus* (New York: Harper and Row, 1964); Cal Samra, *The Joyful Christ* (New York: Harper and Row, 1986); and John W. Drakeford, *Humor in Preaching* (Grand Rapids: Zondervan, 1986).

Chapter 5: We Preach to Be Understood

1. Since this isn't a textbook on hermeneutics, I'll not deal with principles of Bible study or how to move from exegesis to exposition. Some books you will want to consider are: Elliot E. Johnson, *Expository Hermeneutics: An Introduction* (Grand Rapid: Zondervan, 1990); Walter C. Kaiser, *Toward an Exegetical Theology* (Grand Rapids: Baker, 1981); Walter

L. Liefeld, *From Text to Sermon: New Testament Exposition* (Grand Rapids: Zondervan, 1984); A. Berkeley Mickelsen, *Interpreting the Bible* (Grand Rapids: Eerdmans, 1963); Ramesh Richard, *Scripture Sculpture* (Grand Rapids: Baker, 1998); Anthony C. Thiselton, *The Two Horizons* (Grand Rapids: Eerdmans, 1980); Keith Wilhite and Scott M. Gibson, eds., *The Big Idea of Biblical Preaching* (Grand Rapids: Baker, 1998); Roy B. Zuck, *Basic Bible Interpretation* (Colorado Springs, Colo.: ChariotVictor, 1991).

2. I take it that producing fruit—a changed life that glorifies God—is the main evidence of conversion. See Matthew 3:7–12; 7:15–27; John 15:1–16; Romans 7:1–6; Galatians 5:22–23.

3. Frederick W. Robertson, *Sermons: Second Series* (London: Kegan, Paul, Trench Trubner and Co., 1900), 94.

4. See Joel Porte, ed., *Emerson in His Journals* (Cambridge, Mass: Harvard University Press, 1982), 301. During a seminary class one day, a student asked me, "When I'm in the pastorate, do I have to spend thirty hours a week on my Greek?" "Who told you that?" I asked. He said, "My Greek professor." "How many churches has he pastored?" was my next question. The answer was, "None." At that point a second student spoke up: "My Hebrew instructor said we have to spend twenty hours on Hebrew!" "Gentlemen," I said, "don't lose your skills with biblical languages. You've worked hard to develop them and it's a shame to waste your gains. But if you spend fifty hours a week on Greek and Hebrew, you'll lose your church." Blessed are the balanced.

5. It's remarkable how many inaccurate statements and biographical myths are attributed to famous people and passed from one preacher or writer to another. *They Never Said It* by Paul F. Boller Jr. and John George (New York: Oxford University Press, 1989) is a dependable resource for checking such things, and you ought to have two or three good quotation books in your library. I recommend Angela Partington, ed., *The Oxford Dictionary of Quotations* (New

York: Oxford University Press, 1992); Robert Andrews, ed., *The Columbia Dictionary of Quotations* (New York: Columbia University Press, 1993); and Rhoda Thomas Tripp, comp., *The International Thesaurus of Quotations* (New York: Thomas Y. Crowell, 1970). When in doubt about a story or quotation, don't use it.

6. Lloyd Perry used to say that the art of expository preaching lay in knowing when to use the wastebasket.

7. See Faris D. Whitesell and Lloyd M. Perry, *Variety in Your Preaching* (Westwood, N.J.: Revell, 1954); Lloyd M. Perry, *Biblical Sermon Guide* (Grand Rapids: Baker, 1970); Charles W. Koller, *Expository Preaching without Notes* (Grand Rapids: Baker, 1962).

8. Haddon W. Robinson, *Biblical Preaching: The Development and Delivery of Expository Messages* (Grand Rapids: Baker, 1980). See also Willhite and Gibson, eds., *The Big Idea of Biblical Preaching*.

9. Jowett, *The Minister,* 133.

10. Alfred Kazin and Daniel Aaron, eds., *Emerson: A Modern Anthology* (Boston: Houghton Mifflin, 1958), 377.

11. H. Grady Davis, *Design for Preaching* (Philadelphia: Fortress, 1975), 245.

12. The thesaurus on your computer program is handy and helpful and I use mine frequently, but it can't take the place of a good dictionary, especially a dictionary of synonyms. Just as soldiers must know their weapons and carpenters their tools, so preachers must know words.

Chapter 6: We Preach to Effect Change

1. John Ciardi and Miller Williams, *How Does A Poem Mean?* 2d ed. (Boston: Houghton Mifflin, 1975), 2.

2. Hopkins, *Charles Simeon of Cambridge,* 62.

3. Skevington Wood, *John Wesley: The Burning Heart* (Grand Rapids: Eerdmans, 1967), 159.

4. This material is adapted from chapter 3 of my book *Be Wise* published by ChariotVictor Publishers, Colorado Springs, Colorado (1983), and is used with permission of the publisher.

5. It's unfortunate that this important passage is preached as though Paul were writing about the Christians building their lives instead of building the local church. While there is a personal application, the basic interpretation forces us to deal with the local church.

6. If 2 Corinthians 3 isn't familiar to you, I suggest you pause now and read it carefully.

7. This inwardness of the Word is a part of the new covenant (Jer. 31:31–34; Heb. 8:8–12).

8. Three veils are involved in the account in 2 Corinthians 3:7–16: the literal veil Moses wore over his face, the veil over the hearts of the Jews that keeps them from seeing Christ in the Old Testament, and the veil we believers must remove when we read the Word and see Christ in it.

9. The Word of God is compared to a mirror not only here in 2 Corinthians 3:18 but also in James 1:22–25.

10. For an explanation of the use of imagination in preaching, see my book *Preaching and Teaching with Imagination* (Grand Rapids: Baker, 1994).

11. Quoted in Stott, *Between Two Worlds,* 238–39. The statement was made by W. Macneile Dixon in his book *The Human Situation.*

Chapter 7: We Preach from the Overflow

1. T. S. Eliot, *On Poetry and Poets* (London: Faber and Faber, 1986), 27.

2. A. T. Robertson, *Word Pictures in the New Testament,* vol. 4 (Grand Rapids: Baker, 1982), 582.

3. Halford Luccock, *In the Minister's Workshop* (New York: Abingdon, 1944), 144.

4. C. S. Lewis quotes this statement in *George Macdonald: An Anthology* (New York: Macmillan, 1947), 113.

5. Spurgeon, *The Metropolitan Tabernacle Pulpit,* vol. 17, 112.

6. Frances Bacon, *Essays of Frances Bacon* (Garden City, N.Y.: Doubleday), 138. You should read his entire essay "On Studies."

7. John Wesley, *The Works of John Wesley,* vol. 5 (Grand Rapids: Zondervan, n.d.), 2.

Chapter 8: We Preach as an Act of Worship

1. William Temple, *Readings in St. John's Gospel,* 1st series (London: Macmillan and Co., 1939), 68.

2. J. I. Packer, *Beyond the Battle for the Bible* (Westchester, Ill.: Cornerstone Books, 1980), 85.

3. Arthur L. Teikmanis, *Preaching and Pastoral Care* (Englewood Cliffs, N. J.: Prentice Hall, 1964), 19.

4. Wesley, *The Works of John Wesley,* vol. 1, 163.

5. Quoted in Frank Cairns, *The Prophet of the Heart* (London: Hodder and Stoughton, 1934), 63–64.

6. Harry Emerson Fosdick, *The Living of These Days* (New York: Harper, 1956), 226–27.

Chapter 9: We Preach Depending on God's Power

1. The references in Acts to growth are: 2:41, 47; 4:4; 5:14; 6:7; 9:31; 11:24; 12:24; 16:5; 19:20.

2. For a stimulating account of what the Holy Spirit can do when a church devotes itself to prayer, see *Fresh Wind, Fresh Fire* by Jim Cymbala, with Dean Merrill (Grand Rapids: Zondervan, 1997).

3. For a study of the importance of character in Christian

ministry, see chapter 1 of Warren W. Wiersbe and David W. Wiersbe, *Ten Power Principles for Christian Service* (Grand Rapids: Baker, 1997).

4. Andrew A. Bonar, *Memoirs and Remains of Robert Murray M'Cheyne* (London: Banner of Truth Trust, 1966), 282.

5. Richard Baxter, *The Reformed Pastor* (New York: American Tract Society, n.d.), 127. This is a classic work that ought to be read and reviewed regularly by every minister.

Chapter 10: We Preach the Message God Gives Us

1. Bonar, *Memoirs and Remains of Robert Murray M'Cheyne*, 36.

2. G. Campbell Morgan, *The Study and Teaching of the English Bible* (London: James Clarke, n.d.), 37.

3. For good examples of thematic sermons that are expositions of texts, see the books by Clovis Chappell and Clarence Macartney.

4. This series was eventually published in my book *Why Us? When Bad Things Happen to God's People* (Grand Rapids: Revell, 1984). There is also a Spire edition from Revell titled *When Life Falls Apart.*

5. See the biographical sermons of Alexander Whyte, George Matheson, Clarence Macartney, and Clovis Chappell. While ministering over *Back to the Bible Broadcast,* I did several biographical series: angry people of the Bible, happy people, the people at Jesus' feet, people whose prayers weren't answered, and so on.

6. See my *Preaching and Teaching with Imagination,* chapter 19.

7. Dorothy Sayers, *Christian Letters to a Post-Christian World,* edited by Roderick Jellema (Grand Rapids: Eerdmans, 1969), 13.

8. Brooks, *Lectures on Preaching,* 90.

9. See Andrew Blackwood, *Special-Day Sermons for Evangelicals* (Great Neck, N.Y.: Channel Press, 1961). This is a fine collection of sermons by gifted preachers, covering not only the Christian Year but also several of the secular holidays. See also Richard Allen Bodey, ed., *Good News for All Seasons* (Grand Rapids: Baker, 1987) and George Sweeting, *Special Sermons for Special Days* (Chicago: Moody, 1977).

10. Catherine Marshall, *A Man Called Peter* (New York: McGraw-Hill, 1951), 230–31.

Chapter 11: We Preach with Imagination

1. For an extended treatment of this theme and a full bibliography, see my book *Preaching and Teaching with Imagination.* See also Thomas H. Troeger, *Imagining a Sermon* (Nashville: Abingdon, 1990); Walter Brueggerman, *The Prophetic Imagination* and *Finally Comes the Poet* (Philadelphia: Fortress, 1978 and 1989); Elizabeth Achtemeier, *Creative Preaching: Finding Words* (Nashville: Abingdon, 1980); and Northrop Frye, *The Educated Imagination* (Indiana University Press, 1964).

2. See the many books by Leland Ryken for help in studying the Bible as literature, including *The Literature of the Bible* (Grand Rapids: Zondervan, 1974); *Triumphs of the Imagination* (Downers Grove, Ill.: InterVarsity Press, 1979); and *The Liberated Imagination* (Wheaton, Ill.: Harold Shaw, 1989).

3. See George Lakoff and Mark Johnson, *Metaphors We Live By* (Chicago: University of Chicago Press, 1980).

4. The word *enticed* in James 1:14 is a picture of bait put in a trap or on a hook.

5. Francis Schaeffer, *Art and the Bible* (Downers Grove, Ill.: InterVarsity Press, 1973), 5.

Chapter 12: We Preach to the Occasion

1. I still think that the best basic guidebook is Andrew W. Blackwood, *The Funeral: A Source Book for Ministers* (Philadelphia: Westminster, 1942). Unfortunately, it's out of print. Other helpful books are: Robert Blair, *The Minister's Funeral Handbook* (Grand Rapids: Baker, 1990); Dan S. Lloyd, *Leading Today's Funerals* (Grand Rapids: Baker, 1997); Granger Westberg, *Good Grief* (Philadelphia: Fortress, 1982); Warren Wiersbe and David Wiersbe, *Comforting the Bereaved* (Chicago: Moody, 1985); Edwin S. Schneidman, *The Suicidal Mind* (New York: Oxford University Press, 1996); Peter Kreeft, *Love Is Stronger than Death* (San Fransisco: Ignatius, 1992); and David W. Wiersbe, *Gone but Not Lost: Grieving the Death of a Child* (Grand Rapids: Baker, 1992).

Chapter 13: We Preach as Part of a Great Tradition

1. Hegel wrote this in the introduction to his *Lectures on the Philosophy of World History.*

2. Unfortunately, later editors have also altered Spurgeon. For a critical appraisal of "The Kelvedon Edition" of Spurgeon's sermons, see appendix 1 of *The Forgotten Spurgeon* by Iain Murray (London: Banner of Truth Trust, 1966). Except for the messages in *A Quest for Souls,* the sermons of George W. Truett suffered a similar fate. See Clyde E. Fant Jr. and William M. Pinson Jr., *A Treasury of Great Preaching,* vol. 8 (Nashville: Nelson, 1995), 137–39.

3. For a helpful sermon study guide, see Andrew Blackwood's excellent anthology *The Protestant Pulpit* (Nashville: Abingdon, 1947), 305–6.

4. This seminal essay is found in volume 21 of Charles Simeon, *Expository Outlines on the Whole Bible* (Grand Rapids: Zondervan, 1956), 287–435.

5. For a survey of the Yale Lectures on Preaching, see Batsell Barrett Baxter, *The Heart of the Yale Lectures* (reprint, Grand Rapids: Baker, 1971) and Edgar DeWitt Jones, *The Royalty of the Pulpit* (New York: Harper, 1951). Like any series involving many lecturers, it varies in quality and quantity from volume to volume; but it's still worth reading. Some of the books are now period pieces, but even antiques have their charm and value.

Index

Hegel, G. W. F., 145
Heralds to a New Age (Aycock), 152
hermeneutics, 158n. 1
Hiltner, Seward, 152
history, 143–46
History of Preaching in Britain and America, A (Webber), 145
Hitler, Adolph, 49
holidays, 121–22
Holy Spirit: dependence upon, 17; enabling by, 38, 106–8; enlightening by, 105–6; equipping by, 105; filling with, 108; hindrance to, 94; power of, 38, 104–5, 106–7; Word of God and, 74–75
Homiletic: Moves and Structures (Buttrick), 152–53
Homiletical Plot, The (Lowry), 153–54
homiletics, 85
homiletics books, 149–54
Howe, Reuel, L., 152
How to Preach without Notes (Koller), 151
Hull, William E., 152
humility, 26
humor, 50

illustrations, 79–82
imagery, 80, 125–27, 131–32
imagination: concerns over, 124; cultivation of, 128–30; illustrations and, 79–80; metaphor and, 125–27; necessity of, 123; uses for, 127–28

immaturity, 71
inadequacy, 103–4
individuality, 143
individuals, 42–43
integrity, 26–27
Internet, 19
In the Minister's Workshop (Luccock), 150
intimidation, 89–90
introductions, 65–68
Ironside, H. A., 117

Jeremiah, 23–24
Jesus Came Preaching (Buttrick), 150
Jesus Christ: adequacy of, 135; duty and, 38–39; historicity of, 33–34; presentation of, 32; present ministry of, 34–35; prophecy and, 35–36
Johnson, Samuel, 46
Johnson, Torrey, 105
Jones, J. D., 148–49
Jowett, John Henry, 48, 60, 149, 150
Joy of Preaching, The (Brooks), 150

key words, 63–64
Koller, Charles W., 60, 150–51

languages, biblical, 56–57, 159n. 4
Larsen, David L., 145
Latimer, Hugh, 102
law, ministry of, 75
lectionary, 120–21

Warren W. Wiersbe is Distinguished Professor of Preaching at Grand Rapids Baptist Seminary and has pastored churches in Indiana, Kentucky, and Illinois (Chicago's historic Moody Memorial). He is the author and editor of more than one hundred books and now focuses his energies on writing, teaching, and conference ministry.